13 INSPIRATIONS @23

THE STORY OF A YOUNG WOMAN WHO SAID NO TO BEING AVERAGE

MADIHA AHMED

Made with ♥ on the Notion Press Platform
www.notionpress.com

For my beloved nation, India.

I will keep striving for a Better Me, a Better India and a Better World.

Dedicated to the Legendary and Fearless, A.H.

Late Abdul Haque Ahmed, my grandfather, my dada, who always stood up and spoke up for what he believed in.

Contents

PREFACE

He Loves Me.

That is what finally gave me the courage to start writing a book that I had been planning since early 2016.

I delayed writing and publishing due to the following reasons :

1. Lack of credibility for my beliefs and methods, if they were effective and led to success in the long run for me and for others.

2. Need to test my projects and feel satisfied as well as a sense of accomplishment while reading my bio at the back of the book.

3. Not enough readers or people aware of it or interested in my story so I didn't know who would read it and get benefitted.

4. Success stories in my life for a publisher to be interested to sign up a contract with me.

5. Lack of time and focus to organize my thoughts and write them down.

6. Laziness, overcoming helplessness, depression and overwhelmed with a lot of things that excited me.

7. My focus on identifying and trying to figure out Man of Dreams characteristics due to society's pressure.

8. All the popularity after the TEDx and the events that followed.

As I felt heavy thinking about the future, thinking about all the potential Man of Dreams, the piling up work and excitement after the promotion at the US-based virtual company I work at and TEDx video's success, after the honours I received for being a good speaker and listener, I was wondering why the book is still pending, why the projects are still pending, why I've lost focus temporarily of the big picture of becoming Woman of my Dreams as I see the need to share my story via videos, my book and my work with the world, why I wasn't developing the modules I said I would!

I realized I was once again thinking like I did at 23 due to adults talking and relatives telling them. I was thinking: "Will who I am, bring me the Man of Dreams, my kind when society puts pressure? I feared ending up with a typical, mediocre and normal man with whom life will be boring, with a life that I'll regret with a typical unproductive life where I'll only be busy cooking food and fights, washing clothes or even doing a job that majority women do that is stable, safe and "for a woman.""

This time, however, the way I dealt with my fears, my thoughts and uncertainties amazed me. I acted like a responsible youth changemaker which was due to my journey of the last two years and what I learned over this period. I realized what worked then, has been working out effectively and successfully over the last few years but now my understanding of these lessons, insights and reflections has become much better due to:

1. People of expertise and experience either suggesting or sharing similar thoughts.

2. Sharing my story with women and men who are successful and their genuine appreciation and critical feedback on my thoughts, beliefs, practices and the person I am.

3. Youth and many people whom I respect and admire were being inspired by me and relating to my story across the world.

Recalling the success and struggles with the reflection and insights, putting together bits and pieces of the last few years journey pumped me up and I said: "He loves me." That is what really matters and the love that really matters.

So, what are those 13 reflections, insights and inspirations in my life that helped me get started two years back at 23 on saying yes to my dreams and start the journey of becoming the Woman of my Dreams?

Time and again when I lose focus or when the focus waivers, when life struggles distract me then these 13 reflections help me to get back on track. They have helped other young people to say yes to their dreams and start the journey of becoming the woman of their dreams or man of their dreams. These reflections gave me clarity on who the Man of my Dreams could potentially be and how I can test and identify to make a better choice in the future when I'm ready.

More than anything, I got the courage to carry on, to not give up amidst the odds or when life throws challenges, to continue the fight for my dreams and fight for becoming the woman of my dreams.

Acknowledgements

I express my heartfelt gratitude to the following people who inspired me to be a better Me to contribute to a better India and better World so far in my journey of life:

1) Allah (Almighty God)- He is the only One that matters and has always been there for me. Over the years I realized as long as I have good intentions and work hard, He will be on my side. I need Him always. Thank you, Allah, for everything.

2) My Family- Parents- Munir Ahmed and Hamida Ahmed who brought me into this world and taught me the importance of quality, for providing for me and being understanding.

My Grandparents from both sides- Late Yusuf Dinath and Maimoonah Dinath and Late Abdul Haque Ahmed and Rukaiya Ahmed for loving me, for "boasting" about me, praying for me and caring for me.

My uncle and aunt, Asif Ahmed and Anisha Ahmed and cousins, Raafay and Aisha Ahmed for being such an important part of my life always.

My Siblings- Muhammad for being a great example of a boy, breaking all stereotypes since childhood, Khadijah for teaching me karate and Halima for her support and feedback.

4) My Mentors for whom I have the most respect and admiration, who helped me grow personally and professionally- Dr. Illora Sen for believing in me and always identifying the great things I did or could do in life, who taught me to look at life as a school, who helped me make wise decisions in life. Dr. Jawwad Patel, my scientist friend and mentor, for being an example of focusing on God to witness miracles in life and not to be a people-pleaser, for the idea of logo and website with madiha.org.

Mr. Steve Kantor for being such a patient, understanding and encouraging CEO. Dr. Sibichen Mathew for the advice and suggestions on my professional life and career. Mrs. N. Chaturvedi and Ms. A. Banerji for believing in me and my leadership at school. Sister Nirmala for identifying the spark in me. Mr. Prakash Nahata for advice on my education. Mr. Iqbal Lala for encouraging me by sharing views as a mindful parent and mentor.

Dr. Anil Pradhan, from OSU, who has always made me logically process my decisions in life, mentored me in some very defining moments of my life. Mr. Arif Hossain, cardio-respiratory physiotherapist at GD Hospital who has inspired me through his knowledge and care for my late grandfather, my interest in geriatrics and helping me figure out the doctor part of The Edu Doctor through his work, leadership and example.

5) My good friends who have been a great support - Advocate Aafreen Perveen for being a call away and always there to help in my social impact work, Khadija Patel for being there whenever I needed a true friend for any area of my life.

6) My colleagues at work- Mr. Md Mohit Khan, like a brother figure and ex-colleague I have learnt a lot from in the events sector, Dr. Farida Khan, ex-colleague who inspired me for work-life balance, Iktisham Ali and Sana Hasnain Rizvi who are like my strong pillars in the company Realpactech and my impact partners in education, learning and development.

I would also like to express my gratitude to some incredible leaders I had the privilege and honour of meeting over the years.

Mrs Rizwana Saiyed, Mrs Priti Joshi, Mr Gladson Peter, Mr Tapan Aslot, Dr Niket Shastri, Mr Pancham Baraiya, Mrs Karen Tsao, Mrs Purvi Mehta, Dr Pattahil Dhanya Menon, Mr Muneer Alwafa, Dr Reeta Bhattacharya, Mr Kirti Patel, Mr Abbas Dadla, Mr Avelo Roy.

PROLOGUE

In early 2016, my life was a mess.

I was lost, broken, hopeless, depressed, with zero resources and connections.

I even wished for death.

I felt betrayed by society, relatives and people I thought were friends and well-wishers.

I felt that a woman being herself, expressing herself, wanting the best for herself and making her choices for her good and good of humanity was a big problem to society.

This is why they won't "let her have it," "do it" or "get it."

I felt female leadership and empowerment were just topics people mostly spoke about, celebrated and felt pride in.

There was very little action on the ground.

According to me, this was due to several reasons:

1. Women mostly preparing and serving "food at the table" only.

2. Women not actively and productively contributing to the "table conversation."

3. Women spending almost the whole time in cooking, cleaning, children's upbringing and thinking balance is difficult, that there is no time for self or society.

4. Women mostly dreaming about Man of Dreams, spending time and effort to achieve that "goal" through shopping, beauty products, partying, social media postings etc.

5. Women not being supportive of other women and being dominating towards some men in their life.

6. Society has made it difficult, often prohibiting and justifying it as a part of or against culture, tradition or religion.

The more women and even men that I saw around me, I told myself: "This is average. Average is boring and that's not going to be me."

I knew that I wanted to be anything but average.

At 23, I didn't know what I wanted but I knew what I didn't want.

I didn't want to be that woman who would spend her days thinking of what food to make and serve. I didn't want to be that woman who was eligible just for a front desk job or marketing or something simple and easy just "suited for a woman."

I didn't want to be a woman who spent her days fighting and arguing with her parents, in-laws, spouse, kids, neighbours. I didn't want to be like those women at the gym or at the airport, young and old, scrolling up and down their mobile screens, discussing which markets and malls to visit, which fashion trends to follow and offers to grab hold of.

I didn't want to be that woman who would say to the next generation: "This is how it has always been. The world is like that."

No. I repeat. "Average is boring and that's not going to be me," I told myself then.

I wanted to be a trendsetter.

I wanted to set the standards.

I wanted to show the world who an empowered woman really is and to give a glimpse into her mind.

The first big God-sent opportunity was in the form of TEDx where my talk was appreciated and inspired people from India, USA, UK, Canada, Australia, Kenya, Nigeria, Pakistan, Sri Lanka, Latin America, Middle East countries, Hong Kong.

I received so many messages from different parts of India from men and women saying: "We see ourselves in you, a common and ordinary person with an extraordinary story and thought process. If you can do it, so can we."

Sometimes this feedback was from total strangers and it was overwhelming for me.

At a Women Leadership Summit, when a boy of class 7 (both his parents were speakers) asked me for autograph and photograph for being sincere, I knew once again that I was becoming the Woman of my Dreams, setting new standards of being a good listener and being a leader by not just speaking but learning and asking good questions that the organizers, speakers and the audience acknowledged.

I knew I was becoming the Woman of my Dreams when men and women of substance respected me, praised and appreciated me. I was attracting my soul tribe and like-minded people who I could not even dream could exist.

I knew I was becoming the Woman of my Dreams when an elderly uncle from the USA who is highly trusted by my family called up and said that he felt proud to see a young woman and from India speaking on social causes so passionately.

Incidents and moments like these gave me confidence and courage to level up my game. I was convinced that I was headed in the right direction of starting my journey towards living a life of purpose and towards becoming the Woman of my Dreams, even if most in the society would object.

I was striving to become a rare breed of a woman who was a trendsetter, setting high standards for women and girls to emulate and for men and the society, in general, to really know who a truly empowered woman is.

Once I started seeing success as a result of the choices I was making, the insights I was developing, the impact I was having- small but deep, I knew it was time finally to write the book after those few years of "wishing and wanting to write my story."

I wanted to write and share the 13 Inspirations and Reflections not because I had a secret formula or perfect recipe or even "perfect algorithm" for success or to becoming Woman or Man of your own Dreams or to saying yes to yourself and no to society or no to being average.

My intention behind writing the book, writing and sharing my story is to help other women and men relate to my life and story, to be inspired to act, to think differently, to make a sincere effort to start becoming their own Woman of Dreams or Man of Dreams and to live a life they are capable of living- enriching, purposeful, impactful and that will heal and contribute to a Peaceful World on a small and big scale, in small and big ways.

When I said no to potential men of my dreams at 23, I said yes to me. I said yes to becoming the Woman of my Dreams and that changed everything.

Here I am on a journey to become the woman of my dreams, who is empowering others and contributing to creating empowered generations to come. As I evolve and get better, the world will evolve and get better.

In this book, I've shared 13 major areas of concern that young men and women face that I faced at 23 and faced earlier too but I didn't pay attention then. I face a lot of these challenges till today but now I know how to deal with many of them in a better way and I'm learning to deal with many of them every day.

I've shared these with many people when they were going through tough times and it helped them. When I undergo challenges, I think about what I wrote and it gives me confidence and courage to not give up or not to settle for less.

As my journey teaches me, as God inspires me to get better and serve Him and humanity better, to improve myself each day for the better, I'll continue to share my Inspirations, Reflections and Story through my work and books in the years to come.

I
Dealing with "them" and what "they" say

The society I live in loves a woman who says yes to their dreams but dislikes and challenges a woman who says yes to Her Dreams.

Society often say: "Why does she need to study more? She has done her basics well. Why does she need to work at all? Her father, husband, brother, son are there to provide for her and support her. Why does she need an identity of her own? She is the daughter of so and so, the wife of so and so, the mother of so and so, the sister of so and so."

When a woman realizes and chooses to be herself, express herself, want the best for herself then there is a problem according to society.

Society says: "She is going out of hand or control."

"We need to get her married so that her freedom is in check and added roles and duties will make her think and act "more responsible."

"Her meetings and coming late has made her this way. She will fall ill. What will people say? Girls from good homes don't go to such places that are such and such."

"Your age is perfect now and good proposals will come. As age increases, good proposals won't come. You will never have everything you're looking for in a person or family. YOU have to make compromises. Think of the "big picture" in this world and hereafter."

"We have "seen more of the world" and we know it's not easy. It's different in lectures and books but real life is different. And you alone can't change the world and neither can your actions."

Seriously? I was not ready to buy that!

The words I shared above are sometimes uttered by family members or relatives, neighbours, community members of the girl or boy.

As a result, moral policing begins and the activities and plans may be challenged and affected as parents may be under pressure and influenced by elders or their peers. If the young woman speaks up or goes against the elders "commands" then she is declared as "disobedient" or "only serving and being good to people outside."

There could be "gentle reminders" of "charity begins at home," that religion, culture or God commands "to obey and respect" parents or elders at ALL times, to "seek permission" before doing anything or going anywhere as it is a matter of safety, concern or the "world outside is bad."

Here are a few reflections on dealing with people especially elders in the family when it comes to you fulfilling your dreams:

Parents are not bad people

Most parents are not bad people or bad at heart even if they get carried away by their own parents, family or peers, relatives, friends or neighbours. They were brought up differently.

Parents say:

"We have seen more of the world."

"We advise you "out of concern" and "desire to have a good life" for you because we "can't see you in pain."

It is important to understand that they were brought up and conditioned not to "question" anything that their elders said or did at least when it mattered. They did whatever their parents wanted. They were used to following the commandments from people without questioning or even reflecting. Most did not even think of standing up for truth in a different and innovative way.

Reflection is something every person must do and that is what religion emphasizes on but most people pick and choose what suits them and their agendas, often ignoring or avoiding things that really are beneficial to all and would be better for them in the big picture.

I realized that in my case, my parents were good people at heart. I was sure of this in my case and for most people that I knew globally. I knew it was the culture and pressure from the people close to them that made them act in a certain way. This realisation was mainly due to my interactions with some of my friends who made me look at parents differently.

My experience and interactions with parents in schools and events as a parent mentor resulted in the insight that parents needed help but they do not trust easily and will not give their time easily. One reason I discovered was the lack of trustworthy or credible people around who can convince them enough on the topic or the lack of the quality of content and presentation.

Schools were most powerful and influential in educating parents as the parents trusted their children's school which was their choice. Schools would not easily allow just anyone to interact with their parents. I am blessed to have that trust. I am grateful to God to be able to keep that trust.

Some parents told me, "Ma'am, please do workshops so that we can process and analyse ourselves better. Sometimes we do things and do not know what we have done to the child."

I had faith in God and I believed that if I keep striving then my elders will realize, respect, understand and appreciate my efforts and striving. I believed that one day their mindset will change. That happened after two years of my starting the journey towards fulfilling my dreams.

My elders gave importance and respect to females working and achieving, encouraging them to participate in events for their growth and happiness, asking for their opinion and trusting it more than they did before.

This could be difficult for most but know that due to striving, powerful intentions and grind, God will help, support and facilitate things for you.

The concept of permission and obedience

Obedience and respect towards elders especially parents is something basic that every religion, culture and even basic ethics teach. However, there are many cultural elements that lead to wrong ideas and beliefs about the concept of parenting and life in general. Sometimes these are confused with religion. This creates problems rather than contributing towards solutions and progress for humanity.

When my "why" started getting clearer and why I said yes to my dreams, why I wanted to be Woman of Dreams then my views, attitude, behaviour and practices starting undergoing a major transformation.

The impact showed in my work with parents in schools and at events when parents connected with me and often wondered: "How come you know parenting when you are not even a parent!"

The way I looked at the parent-child relationship changed, the way I would honour, respect, love and care for my elders changed. Even with hurtful faces and tears, words of extreme concern politely or in a loud tone, I was focused, I could talk to myself about it, I could deal with it and that too without feeling guilty or hurt or depressed for very long.

I would be the first one to start talking, smile or get back to normal after a heated moment or discussion with elders as I knew they were good people otherwise and it was their concern as well as the external pressure that made them act the way they did.

Also, they needed to see me striving to be different from other youth. An example could be by not responding the typical way most people would respond like not talking or being upset for long or waiting for others to take the first step towards friendship or reconciliation. They needed to see a better example in me.

I would either say or do something to make elders and loved ones feel special in spite of the differences and contrasting beliefs. I would think aloud and have conversations with other people around them so that they would know that I was striving hard in every way and to make them aware about my thought process and also how I acted in public through my Facebook posts and videos.

Yes, obedience to elders is something that God commands but above this is obedience to God and there is no compromise and forgiveness in this case if you don't take action and mend your ways.

I realized God created me and with a purpose. When I live to the fullest and invest first in myself and then invest in building and helping people, I will fulfill that purpose. I realized God created me with certain skills, gifts and blessings. He sent different people and experiences my way and I'm sure He doesn't make things happen just like that. I'm sure there is a hidden purpose and meaning behind everything that happens.

I didn't want to be buried in the grave with all of that unutilized. What a waste that would be!

Your "why" will give you courage

I often thought about people who did something wrong without seeking permission and knowledge of elders.

If those who did wrong or evil actions, if those who committed crimes could use their brains and be brave then why couldn't I use my brains and be brave for my life's purpose?

Why did I need permission? My policy and attitude changed from seeking permission to informing. I researched and reflected, I reasoned thoroughly and at times consulted my mentors and my close friends.

I often think about why I said yes to my dreams for the first time at 23 and recall past incidents when God helped me as my why was getting clearer.

Upon my society's concern every now and then about getting married as "it was my age" but I didn't want to yet, I had my why clear and that's why I had the courage to say no without worrying about future. I did not want to marry for the reason they wanted.

No one will accompany you to the grave

I started thinking about the verses and sayings of Prophet Muhammad (peace be upon him) that I studied since my teens on death and legacy. I realized that I wasn't going to live forever and when I am buried then my wealth and materialistic belongings, my family and loved ones will leave me alone.

Only my deeds will accompany me to the grave, my deeds and actions with powerful intentions that will determine my future and ultimate fate. The fears and critics, the taunts and challenges, society's opinions about me will mean nothing then.

I thought to myself that I must collect enough good deeds- Good deeds that will go with me to the grave and ensure a better Hereafter as well as deeds that I'll be remembered for, in the world as a legacy. If I don't collect them from now then it might be too late and I'll regret in the Hereafter more.

Wanting greater good for elders

As I started focusing on changing myself for the better, leading by example and taking responsibility for being more ethical than the society I grew up in then I realized that it isn't always the elders or society that thinks and wants greater good for youth.

Sometimes it's the other way. I told myself: "Today, my elders will be unhappy, sad or angry and hurt because of me. They are all getting carried away by the culture and society. The same society that opposed me, who at one point of time called up my folks to complain now applauds, appreciates, respects and wants to be associated with me."

This is the same society that now talks about me as a trendsetter, as a woman setting very high standards. I get messages saying that they find my posts and videos helpful. I get suggestions that I must use vernacular to connect with more women in India.

I also told myself: "Madiha, all this pain and struggle, hurt and suffering is part of life as life is a test. In the Hereafter and maybe in this world, God will heal them and eventually they will understand the wisdom and reasoning behind your actions, choices and decisions. Moreover, Madiha remember, you learned about children being an ongoing charity for parents and elders after they leave this world. So if you are striving and focusing on creating a better world, being more ethical than the world and society you grew up in and for that, gathering the courage to challenge stereotypes and "disobeying" elders of the society in certain things or refusing to take permission in certain things then you are doing more good than wrong. Of course there are good things they do and say, take those but filter out the not so productive ones."

I must not give up and carry on striving to be an example.

Concerns about safety

Elders often have concerns about safety as their protective nature and concerns were very prominent and necessary in their child's early years from the time they were born till their teens. They feel the attachment and that they don't want to cut off till either they leave the world or till their children leave this world.

The concept of safety many a times revolves around having full knowledge of physical activities and movements of children or other people. This is why society has messed up adults and there are social issues. That is why there are so many problems in the world that results in so much suffering and we fail to arrive at effective and long-lasting solutions.

When my 9-year-old brother was kidnapped, my whole family was worried and crying except me. On my way to the police station, I prayed to God: "God, Muhammad is not mine or ours. He is Yours. You created Him and to You he will return. I can't protect him. I'm weak and my knowledge is limited, so is my wisdom. Wherever he is, whoever he is around, please protect him physically, mentally and spiritually. When he is back please make him a strong boy in every way. Please don't let him be hurt or allow him to be broken as he has lots to offer to the world and humanity. He is so sensitive and caring, so empathetic and a problem solver. He is a visionary who has big dreams and always willing to learn and serve."

At night, all elders were crying and praying, some went for searching but I did my best to help from home online and kept having that faith along with hard work and good intentions.

He did come back in the morning around 7 AM. God protected him. God heard my prayers.

I left my boy to His Care, the best there is and could be. My brother had gone to pray when he was kidnapped. His and our intention as a family was good. This incident actually made my conviction stronger that society's concern about safety was not that big.

In spite of talking about faith and religion and God, I always saw faith lacking in action in most people. I wasn't the most religious person. I prayed namaz and recited Quran as much as I could without rushing it just to complete it. I always believed in intentions and actions.

Your tribe matters

When society and my own people were being a test for me, I realized the need for people, my people, my kind of people to help me improve my growth game.

I realized the need for genuine people who I could hang out (mostly virtually) with, with whom I could have honest conversations with, heart to heart and soul to soul talks with, without the fear of being judged. Virtually because it helps to stay connected and save time, to remain productive and focused, to give each other the space and grow better while having better understanding of meaningful relationships.

It isn't easy at all to find your tribe. Trust me.

I never had very successful long-term friendships in the past in my school or college. Then I was mostly surrounded with people who were people pleasers and who cared a lot about "log kya kahenge" (what will people say). I was surrounded mostly by people who followed the crowd and wanted to fit in, who wanted to follow trends and who thought that the "world is like that and this is how it is."

I had no time for friends outside of school or college because I had lots of things to do and I didn't like bunking or have a relationship with boys for the reasons they did. I didn't like doing what everyone did. I knew I wanted to be different and I was that way but that resulted in me paying a heavy price each time.

And each time in spite of the loss of people, the lack of sense of belonging and lack of things for a typical person my age would want, for the reasons they did, I stuck to my core and principles.

I loved loneliness and spending time with myself in spite of being an extrovert.

In college, for cricket, I practiced in winters, very early morning, all alone at the stumps. For breaks, I would eat quickly either towards the beginning or end of it to be able to practice or do any activities I wanted.

Amidst the lonely time, I made different connections and bondings, with God, with nature, with the vibes of struggling and successful souls around me while I observed it all. Most importantly, my connection with my inner self was getting stronger and clearer.

a) Connection with God

God was the only One I didn't need appointment from, who was always there for me- sometimes late night and sometimes early morning, sometimes while lying on the bed and sometimes while in the washroom, sometimes while I was walking on the road or sometimes when all alone amidst a huge crowd.

Any time I needed His help and guidance, I just had to remember Him. I would talk to Him through prayers like namaz or through gazing at the sky, through a silent talk closing my eyes or writing on paper to express myself or even Facebook as a post or poster.

What was beautiful was that I just said the words or sometimes I could not and He still understood.

And upon seeking Help, Guidance and Answers, He showed His responses through the turn of events, through a person sent to mentor or guide me in unexpected ways and places and times, through the weather-raindrops, thunder, clouds movement, through birds or insect movement, through an article, video or post or comment, through the few people I called my soul tribe who always stood by me, cared for me and gave me honest feedback.

I got answers sometimes immediately and sometimes eventually.

One thing was constant was that I got answers and He did respond when I called out to Him, any time, any day while always striving and having good intentions and seeking forgiveness when erring.

b) Connection with Nature

My earliest lessons on social change and life were through my connection with nature. There was one time when after my photosynthesis classes in college, I was on the way to my house. My car was stuck in traffic and I saw on my left a tree that was growing on a ground but higher than the rest, quite unlike others and standing out. The sun rays were falling on the trees and the sight looked beautiful.

I told myself: "If these sun rays would fall and strike just the superficial layers of the leaves then food (glucose) will not be produced. Life giving, Oxygen will not be the outcome. It's only because sunlight strikes the chlorophyll that is situated internally, that the change happens and glucose and oxygen are the result."

I said "Yes! This is social change."

The sunlight strikes the internally situated chlorophyll that is activated, food is produced by the leaf and then this is circulated to other parts of the plant. Oxygen is given out by the plant that makes life possible. If I want to bring social change then I must allow the inspiration and the light to enter my heart and transform it. When my heart will change, I'll change for the better and the way I think and feel, speak and act will significantly change. Then I must not keep that inspiration and light to just myself. I must take and spread the light in the world around me.

All this I must do while my roots are well nourished by learning and exposing myself to beneficial things and keeping myself away from unproductive things and actions. That is how change will come and I'll continue to strive for a better me and a better world.

c) Connection with the vibes of souls around me

Time and again, in spite of being an extrovert, I withdrew myself from people to preserve myself- seeking alone time for reflection, reducing time and energy spent on and with people who would make me less productive through hangout, parties and social gatherings.

I stopped talking to some people. I quit some groups. I blocked or ignored some people.

These were people who made me unproductive and with the help of my close friends, I was guided better to understand who matters and who does not. I understood that being a social changemaker, I would meet lots of people but I would have to carefully choose people around me.

My close friends helped me understand the importance of "saying no" to things that do not matter and "saying no" to people who would drain me out of my energy and productivity. I learned to utilise my time and efforts better as I desired and aimed for legendary and inspiring life. I am determined to make it happen.

I learned to say no so that I could focus on striving for a Better Me, Better India and Better World.

I made errors but I learned fast.

I realized that the best thing I could do to serve India and humanity was to preserve myself, to invest in myself, to keep myself sane and intact and only when I'm full and my cup is full, can I pour in others cups and help them. Only then will I contribute to a better and happy family, a better and prosperous nation, my India!

I tried not to have a lot of time alone because my extrovert nature wanted me to be amidst people and my work put in me the desire to observe people, learn from them so that I could understand and deliver and serve better.

In college, I spent some time in the week, pretending to study in rooms where girls would hang out a lot during free periods like the common room, classes where there were no lectures just so I would know what girls talk about, what bothers them, what their challenges are.

Even while traveling or in gatherings, I observe people and try to absorb and understand the frequency of souls around me- at some point of time it was all virtual and since the last 1 and half years a balance of virtual and in-person.

I was getting good at understanding and identifying the frequency and vibes of souls around me both ways- virtual and in-person.

Tribe- Who? Why? How?

So who is your tribe? How do you know they belong to your tribe?

Start distancing yourself from unproductive activities, people and places. Only then will your tribe find you and you will find your tribe.

Be honest and true to yourself. Always. Only then will you start attracting people who will be the same and you'll connect.

Share parts of your life and test people to trust them or to see if you and they are aligned or it's worth investing in that relationship. Trust your gut feeling. It will guide you. In case you get negative vibes, process them, go to their depths, give it time, accept and act on them wisely.

Join genuine virtual and physical groups that align with your interests to meet like-minded people and to exchange ideas, learn and grow. Interact, respect others and question politely with a spirit of learning without making others feel inferior or pulling them down. Talk about things that matter to you and honestly, without the need to be applauded and to voice out your concerns.

I have had this attitude towards the society that parents have towards children: "I love you and care for you. I want to make things better for you."

Remember, it's okay to stand up to the society and speak up against it so that you can stand up for it and speak for it.

Blood tribe and Soul tribe

Too often we are so attached to our blood tribe, that's connected through the blood that we may end up feeling guilty, end up making wrong choices and decisions as their concerns and love may talk us out of our dreams.

Many a times they make you believe and prevent you from achieving what you truly deserve for work, for relationships, for marriage, for impact.

It is very difficult to say no or yes or turn down what your loved ones, what the immediate family wants and says, because you feel you owe them, because you were raised by them, that you were made and brought up by them, you deserve to respect, love and serve them. You don't want to see them cry, hurt or in pain at least because of you.

I was always thinking this and that's why I started feeling the need to find that tribe. I had started becoming the woman of my dreams and that's why I feel and believe I found my soul tribe of friends, mentors, mentees. Talking to them gave me clarity and courage. They asked me good questions and I started seeing things more clearly.

With clarity, I got the courage to act on what I knew was right and that was being true to myself, God and humanity. That helped me make decisions I did not regret and gave me long-term gain. Happiness and Peace, Gratitude and Satisfaction topped that list.

Sometimes there were lows and highs even with my soul tribe but we believed in being honest and true to God, to each other and to ourselves. We believed in collaborating, clarifying, apologizing, discussing and striving to make things better and ourselves better first.

In spite of virtual friendships and mentorship, we didn't hold back or betray each other. We shared the smallest and biggest things that happened or mattered to us which we couldn't share with our blood tribe.

On Relatives

Relatives can be a great support during difficult times and at the same time a source of great difficulty in life.

When it comes to a woman and her dreams and many a times a man and his dreams, it is the relatives who can put great pressure on the family of the woman- to stop them from studying or work, to plan and plot the marriage, to manipulate and to misguide the family with emotional, cultural, family and ancestors related statements to be able to influence or force them to act according to their wishes.

There was a time when I loved greeting, meeting and connecting with relatives but as I started living the life of my dreams while fighting big internal battles, these relatives started bigger unnecessary battles.

Some of them who created problems in my life few years back, were the same people who now wanted the world to know their connection with me, who praised me, who wanted to involve me directly in some work or the other and if that failed then they tried to take the channel of being an intermediate party for marriage proposals. I knew these traps and plans, therefore I acted accordingly.

There were some relatives who would call up my folks and complained that I was online at 3 PM and 3 AM on Facebook. They said that I shouldn't go out too much as the world outside was unsafe for children and women. These were the same people who later commented or said: "Keep it up. Proud of you. Keep going on." There were some relatives who were traditional and couldn't see other women doing differently, some because they never had the courage to ask or do or they were of those who believed and forced on others only- "This is how it has always been. The world is like that. The theory is different but real life doesn't work that way. You'll regret it at some point." There were elders who said: "If only we "stopped" her back then she wouldn't have the "guts" to speak up. How can she not listen to her elders? You have to "listen" to us. Don't go there. Work or study from home only. You've always been such a "good" girl, what's happened now?"

How to deal with relatives?

Strive to have great clarity about your purpose in life so that your confidence in your work and cause grows, to speak up for yourself. I was very clear about my "why" and I was only doing this because all "polite limits" were crossed and if I was polite always then I'll lose the battle or be forced or the actions and plans would be taken behind my back.

After talking or explaining or defending loudly, calm down and take out time to explain to them the big picture. Don't allow the conversation to be dragged or get too long. Cut it short. You may just have to repeat everything again and again which is a waste of energy. This energy can be better channelized for your dreams, hard work with prayers.

Total isolation from family isn't practical and possible most of the time so plan time and life accordingly.

Many of my friends who went through similar challenges suggested that moving to another city or staying in a hostel helped them. There was "less wastage of time and energy" in arguments or fights.

I did not want to do that. I did not want to do what they did.

I told myself: "Madiha, whatever steps you take and the path you create or follow, other thousands of girls and even boys must be able to replicate. Your problem, your challenge is common and faced by thousands. Do what those thousands can follow and do, seeing your example."

So, if I wasn't moving out then inside the home where everyone was mostly concerned about me, where they kept asking me questions or talking to me about my present and future, worrying often, how did I manage to deal with them and carry on work?

Listen to something productive with your earphones so that they get used to seeing you with it. They will gradually learn to give you space while complaining a lot initially and then eventually leading to reduced complaints. Also, if they are talking about you then listen sometimes but ignore sometimes, otherwise you'll be too overwhelmed to work and focus.

No one can plan for you or against you until God wants that. If you trust Him and are sincere then He will be on your side. There would be nothing to worry about.

Plan your hours during the day and night for work so that you are mostly productive. Include hours of housework and helping the family so that they feel happy and you get to spend time with them. If at that time they start to talk of things you don't want or that gets you overwhelmed then be patient as much as you can otherwise either start talking about something else or bring up work in another room or part of the house, make a call.

Remember the big picture. In case that doesn't help then do express your feelings and let them know politely but firmly that you don't want that conversation.

Have a weekly to-do list as it's more effective than a daily to-do list. Breakdown the weekly list into a daily list and try your best to accomplish as much as you can daily. Just in case you are unable to then carry on the next day but completing it in a week.

Take out some time in the day or week to talk to your folks or do something that makes them happy but which is possible, practical and not against your principles and values. When any of my folks started the topic and tried to talk me out of my dreams then I'd say: "This topic isn't worth of my time, thought and energy. Please let's not talk about this. It does not bring benefit to humanity or country or family."

Initially, there will be times when work will be taken from you even if you want to do it and hints given to you to choose between housework or work. You can be told: "You leave it. We will do it." There could be times when you would have to answer calls and while you talk, they could be talking loudly or doing what you wouldn't want them to. I would sometimes run from one room to the other. But gradually things became easier. I chose to pay attention enough to understand and find a strategy to deal with it but not too much to let it affect my work or focus.

Later, I was told to choose work and delegate housework to a maid. I then said: "That is also my work and this is also my work. I am an empowered woman. I will do both."

Being more ethical than them- I always tried to identify where the relatives and my folks were not being "truly ethical" and still preaching a lot.

Often I found that what they didn't practice was more important than what they preached. What they emphasized as important was not as important as what they ignored. They may bring religion or culture into the conversation. I wasn't worried anymore because I started improving my practices and striving to be more ethical than the society I grew up in.

So for example, if a person said: "If you don't listen to me or if you go then I'll die of stress in old age," then I'd say: "I can't be foolish to end my life or move out because things here are tough. That's like being an escapist and a loser. Also, death sees no age. Today or tomorrow my journey on earth could end too but I must be ready for that and live to the fullest so that I have no regrets at all."

Make your day productive and indulge in productive activities that include your entertainment and conversations you have. Keep yourself motivated and busy with good things and good people.

Conversations- Avoid conversations that will lead to conflict, hatred, unproductivity at a personal, family, societal or world level. I started avoiding conversations that were about putting people down or criticising them, disgracing or discriminating against a person or group.

I avoided conversations that brought about depression, sadness, hopelessness, misery and negative thoughts. My focus was on productive conversations and living a productive life that filled my life and others lives with hope, positive energy and motivation to think and act big.

Prayer- Pray for your relatives or folks that God guides them to a productive way of living, that their hearts find peace, consolation and God heals them of hurt, ill-feelings and worrying about you and the society, that they find courage to see and that they support that which is beneficial to humanity and not just themselves or their children or family. That too in the short term and long term.

Whatever I have shared in this chapter has helped me deal with my folks in an effective way and I'm seeing a positive change gradually.

REFLECT:

1. What are the major challenges that you have faced from people around you when it comes to saying yes to your dreams or when it comes to becoming the man or woman of your dreams?

2. What action will you take after reading this chapter on "Inspiration 1" to deal with them and what they say?

II

Failed. Rejected. Now what?

Our society hasn't taught individuals to deal with failure and rejection and that is its greatest failure.

Society wants to see success, it glorifies success, respects success and this definition of success is all messed up.

An example is a rejection by a school or college, company, a person for marriage or friendship results in prolonged periods of depression, low self-esteem and in some cases suicides or mental health issues or diseases, lack of sense of purpose among kids, teens, youth, adults and elderly.

Everyone is affected by this failure on society's part.

Since I was a child, I have seen rejection. The "best" schools in the city rejected me until after the class 10 selection exams, when I got admission in the best and top girl's school, Loreto House in Kolkata on merit.

The "best" colleges I wanted rejected me until I joined Shri Shikshayatan College where I started cricket as an official tournament. The "best" organizations and companies rejected me until I joined Lifebushido, a US-based virtual company where I'm the Triangle Leader working with US and Globals recruits and new hires.

I joined as a Volunteer Catalyst at +Acumen, the world's school for social change and was selected as a Local Expert for an Indo-US collaboration-Women in STEM Roadshow 2018 by the U.S Department of State and a project of The Ohio State University.

I am a speaker and influencer at SpeakIn, Knuts and India Speakers Bureau when all my life I was afraid of the mic and never got opportunities due to various reasons. I am planning for my second TEDx.

I faced rejections from the "best" males I thought were best for work or friendship or mentorship and today I'm blessed to have the best there could be in the world, who respect me for who I am, for who I'm striving to be and they are my partners and allies in creating impact.

Today after years of facing rejection, I've learned some important lessons and developed my own insights and strategies to deal with it.

Redefining best

I have realized that the way society has defined best hasn't always been the right or the best one.

So often the definition of best is non-inclusive, restricting, discriminating, unethical and standardized. As a teacher, here are my reflections on some of the above mentioned words and phrases:

Non-inclusive

This means that not everyone can be the best, that only if you have certain privileges, you can be the best.

As a trainer, teacher, parent and youth mentor, I have always encouraged others to do their best, to give them hope that they can be the best if they strive and then the best will come to them.

You don't need to belong to a certain caste, community, gender, religion, geography, educational or professional background or from family with certain privileges to be the best version of you, to stand out for being proudly you, to be the best there is possible and then to strive to help the rest to be their best.

Once a scientist from the USA asked me about what my dad did, another time a boutique owner and some friends whose parents were in state governance. They all wondered how I took such a different path and how I created my identity when my father was into plastic toys business and such a humble personality.

Even in social circles, I sometimes hesitated because of strange reactions I got early on but then I started realizing that he was best in a different way and that his traits were in me but I chose and allowed myself to work towards the best version of me in a different way. My dad and his generation had different ideals and he chose to be with his family rather than a good life just for himself abroad. He had social pressures and he did what was important then and good for his family. People in his generation were "trained" differently but today's generation is different.

I took the decision of choosing India when there were opportunities in plenty for me in the west. I did something similar but I wanted to take the family legacy to a new level. I am doing it. My dad's best features are his compromising nature, not having any extreme unethical or unhealthy practices, his love and concern for his family, for poor and rich. He wakes up early and avoids late night work or staying out of home. He encourages my mom, my sisters and me to have a voice and opinion. He supports us all. He loves his mum. This is the same man who my other folks called conservative but he is the hero really. He doesn't speak about female empowerment but his actions reflect it.

The definition of best that society gave didn't fit dad but he was more successful and better in some ways than those who appeared to be successful and spoke but didn't practice and their actions didn't reflect their beliefs.

When my mom or other female elders tell me about their early years or youth, I often think about why society wanted history to repeat. It wanted me to follow in the footsteps of the females older to me in my family. As it is with the education system and is the "way of the world," society wanted mass scale production of the same kind. My mom's best characteristics are maintaining good relation with elders on both sides of her family, serving them, giving her best for almost everything- food, clothes and lifestyle choices. She was an analytical thinker when it came to making choices-business and home-related work. One of the things she would tell me and my siblings often since my teens is: "Never copy. Always be original. Others should copy us."

I think that has become so ingrained in me that I decided and chose to be a trendsetter in different areas of my life, when elders would tell their children to be like me, I'd say: "Learn from me and from everyone, the best that they or I have and filter it to use in your own context. I pray you become better than me and the best you can be."

Restricting

This is to say that to be the best you have to have a lot of criteria, a long list of characteristics, you have to follow steps and processes, you have to score high on a checklist.

To be the best version of you, to be the best you can be, I believe you must identify your talents, skills, strengths and weaknesses either on your own or with the help of your mentors, teachers, parents, trusted persons and delve deeper into your soul to identify what problems you want to solve in the world.

I learned this when I reflected on a video shared by my close friends. I realized that's the path I had been following since last few years, identifying social problems and striving to align my talents, skills and passion to solve them in collaboration with like-minded people and organizations.

When you do that you can live a fulfilling life as what you have and what the world needs comes together to help you realize your purpose in life. This leads to more happiness, more profits, more personal satisfaction and more social impact.

What you have of talents, skills and knowledge must not remain that way always. In fact every week or at least month, you must feel the need and act to upgrade yourself, to be more valuable and get beneficial knowledge, acquire skills so that you stay unique and more impactful over the years to come.

Standardised

This is to say that in spite of having flexibility, the definition of best should be the same for all.

In reality, however, it varies from person to person, case to case but certain core principles must be identified and lived up to (at least striving towards it) to live a principle-oriented and purpose-driven life.

To be the best I could be, to help me eliminate what was not best for me, to help me keep striving to be the best version of myself, here is what I found helpful. It is based on reflections on everything I learned and observed by studying articles, books and people globally:

Being true to yourself

Due to challenging times and the challenges offered by people very close to you, you may have lots of twists and turns, you may have to say a few harsh words or cause pain to eliminate pain and corruption in the long term.

The way I analyzed failure and rejection was different from the way the more "matured" and "wise" society saw it and analyzed it. When they saw something as a rejection by a boy or family, I saw a miracle and opportunity that I kept asking God for while striving hard- a country I didn't want to live in forever or serve for the rest of my life, leaving my own beloved nation. I saw them as a means to stay motivated to plan my life goals not based on a person or place in India but to think and act local, national and global.

I saw the "rejections" as "redirections" to polish my goals and life plans, to have a solid scientific introduction suited to my personality that impressed a lot of people. I used them to get more clarity on what work I must do and for whom and how. My vision and mission improved a lot.

There were times when I really wanted to eat or buy something or go to certain places but I took a step back on several occasions and on being asked I said no to them so that I could say yes to my dreams, to give more time to my dreams, on working and improving myself, to be fit for it and work on its model and method of working. My purpose and cause were more important than anything else.

Being true to God

After realizing the need to be true to myself, I realized I could deceive myself sometimes and make adjustments as per my needs, wants and desires.

A mentor and scientist friend, helped me understand this concept even better even though I was living the principle over the years. He made me realize that to keep being successful, impactful, on the receiving end of miracles from God, to keep doing your best for society, nation and humanity, it's important to stay true to God.

Whatever you do must not prick your conscience and that you must be able to share with everyone. I agree with him but there have been cases where the youth were not able to tell parents or some elders. I realized that that trust and bonding varied due to generation gap, mindset, culture, upbringing, company of friends and education that these adults had.

To share everything all the time didn't make sense as the bigger vision and mission would be hindered and sacrificed and that is the greatest wrong that can be done to yourself and humanity.

This would result in more harm than good for you, the society and nation you want to contribute positively to and towards a better world.

So remember, if you can talk to God about it and sleep at night peacefully without fear or guilt, with the bigger goal in mind then that's enough.

Feedback and Failure

I realized the importance of feedback through Lifebushido's concept of Kaizen and +Acumen's course on Udemy on Radical Candor by Kim Scott.

When failure and rejection occur in life, it is natural and human to feel low and demotivated, discouraged and hopeless but if your "why" in life is clear then both rejection and failure will be your friends and you'll learn to develop strategies and use them to build you rather than break you.

From exploring one marriage proposal that didn't work out, I learned about myself, that my desire to serve my country and people was greater than my desire to just a have a life of luxury for myself in the west. I learned that I wanted to be the person, the kind that the west would think as best and look at as a trustworthy source for cause or collaboration in my country. From exploring another proposal, I realized that I preferred a spouse from the science or tech background, intellectual but more to my liking and with more common interests. I understood that a doctorate didn't necessarily reflect education and open-mindedness. I realized I respected a self-made person more.

From my experience with an organization, I realized I wasn't happy with the way male-dominated organizations worked for females. I wanted to start my own organization that was led by me and a few other females at the top and where men worked too. From another experience, I had a tough time after the interview and in dealing with my elderly folk's moods and the horrible things told to me and emotional blackmailing but I learned to stand my own ground and alone. Then dad and mom supported too.

I realized that I wanted the freedom to be and do on my own. I didn't like restrictions in work as I would lose creativity and innovation sparks.

I learned a lot about feedback from the +Acumen course on Udemy by Kim Scott on Radical Candor that is helping me in personal and professional life till today. I took this course towards the end of 2017. I started realizing that most people don't know how to give feedback- society either goes to one extreme of praising or the other extreme of insulting and pointing flaws or it gets very vague and general and the feedback has no meaning and serves no purpose.

I learned to give feedback:

-that showed appreciation and at the same time challenged

-that was specific

Appreciation and Challenge

Whether it was during teaching or public speaking or training or coaching, my interactions with people in general or even with myself, I became particular about what I learned from the short course on Radical Candor.

When it came to teaching, I'd give feedback like this: "Sidra and Kaif, you're both doing very well. Could you try one more time or write another rhyming word?"

When it came to public speaking, my memories and incidents from Surat visit, I recall giving feedback like: "Nitin, good thinking. Good point. Could you extend this concept a little beyond the topic?"

When it came to my interaction with my own family members and elders, I'd say: "Yes, this looks fine. What are the other options for you? What if such and such thing was done?"

When it came to self-talk and feedback to self, I'd say: "Madiha, you've done it. You are doing well but this isn't going to be easy at all. You must do it better this time."

"Hey, Madiha! You can't be a loser and give up. You've come so far. You have lots of potential. You were not so good this time but you will need to invest more to get and be the best next time."

Specific Feedback

I seriously find it a waste of time and energy to write only "very good" or "brilliant" most of the time as it's not effective feedback.

I recall giving feedback to two boys- one fellow member who spoke during Network Capital meet and another a video editor for a Girl Power Empowerment event. To one of them, I said: "Your knowledge on the topic was really good and even your knowledge of the connected or related topics. Your energy and passion were visible. You must, however, remember as a Speaker you must be in control of the crowd and therefore ignore or skip questions that aren't related to the topic even if elders ask."

To the other, I said: "The frame is very good and the sound effects of the video too."

Reflection before and after Feedback

Feedback must be given or received not just for the sake of it but it must be accompanied by reflection before and after it.

Reflection before Feedback

Many a times I've seen people wanting to give feedback to pull down another person or show themselves superior or knowledgeable or to humiliate another person or take past revenge.

A common example is elders doing that to youth or youth doing that to elders. I've seen elders giving feedback to youth to point out how careless they are, that they don't understand the world yet and that they will regret someday, that they wouldn't have been granted permission to be "this way" now. This happened in my case when it came to dreams, study or work or marriage.

I've seen youth telling elders how unfair or outdated they are, that they never understand or they mentally tortured them. I've spoken to elders impolitely too but most of the time, I try to think of the big picture before feedback, like if out of respect I stayed silent or said something untrue/ unfair then I'm doing more harm than good to humanity so feedback could and would have to be bit firm and raw so that truth and justice prevail. So that I stay sane and preserved to serve humanity.

I realized I had to stand up for myself to stand up and speak up for humanity.

I quickly got normal too if this topic wasn't touched upon by elders again so that they also avoided repetition after listening and watching me, for the next time.

Reflection before giving feedback may be quick or delayed depending on sensitivity and urgency and cause. It varies from person to person, case to case and what's important is that it must be out of concern and good wishes for another person and benefit for humanity at large.

Reflection after Feedback

After receiving feedback, it might be that you are too happy and excited or too sad and demotivated. You may be tempted to react or respond immediately.

I believe filtering of feedback is very important. This is how I filter feedback when given to me:

i) Who has given feedback?

It's important to consider who the feedback is coming from- positive or negative. Near and dear ones may give feedback due to love and concern as well as personal jealousy or own personal issues.

An example is a female elder telling younger females to not work or study or do a certain thing based on societal pressure that existed in her own time. Another example is a male elderly saying to a young female that he was like her in his youth and took hasty decisions too that he regrets today. A successful entrepreneur boss who has the inclination towards social work giving advice to his mentee and employee that she should do more paid work at this stage and have focused goals. A successful teacher, wife, mom, daughter and colleague advising her young female relative to fight the society's battles and to stand up for herself and to keep striving.

ii) Content of the feedback

Is the feedback too much or unrelated and maybe not explained well to your context?

Is there too much positive that sounds and feels like flattering or too much negative that sounds and feels like an attack? Is the content attacking or pulling down a person or group or is it pertaining to the cause and improving something or solving a problem?

Will it make you happy now or even 5-10 years later if you followed their advice and paid a lot of attention to their feedback?

iii) Tone of feedback

Listen well. If you get the vibe and feel it isn't sounding right- trust your gut feeling and heart and give it a chance. Reflect a bit and see if someone you loved the most and trusted said the same, would you consider or pay attention or give it some thought?

If your own mood isn't good, if you're angry or exhausted, don't think too much to filter it immediately. Leave it for another time when you feel better or happier. You may draw more positive lessons out of a negative feedback too.

We are all humans

Often while dealing with failure and rejection, society tags either one who rejects or one who is rejected as bad. The rejected and rejector could be an organization or a person for study or work or for marriage. Society will tell you to distance yourself, cut off ties, speak badly and be happy at the downfall or when tragedy strikes the rejector or the rejected.

In most of my cases, that is what I have seen the elders doing for years. I knew I had to be more ethical than the society I grew up in and I had to be the winds of change so I told them to invite a family for our family occasion. It's okay to be professional friends with a family or a person with whom things didn't work out.

A friend once said something: "Every social changemaker is part of my family." I continued to greet them during festivals or liking their posts.

Neither the rejector nor the rejected are bad people according to me no matter what the society says or forces me to believe. I believe they are all humans and each of them will do something good and bad things that the world may or may not know about but God knows it all.

He knows what's in our hearts and minds even if we see signs and "symptoms"- some of which may be true and some false. Let's give others a chance or at least not go to the extent of revenge, hurt and personal attack.

I believe in praying first for myself if I'm hurt or upset due to "being not good enough" and being told things that reflect it is a "curse to be empowered" or when I see others hurt because of me and my determination to "not fit in."

I then pray to God for my loved ones who sometimes in spite of being older or matured don't get the big picture. I pray for them that they are healed and that God gives them patience to not hurry or worry or act out of hurry or worry and end up causing more harm than good to humanity and for generations to come.

The common reaction and response by the rejector and rejected is to give in and settle for little and for something they don't deserve. It's not easy when there is pressure from inside or outside. But not giving in to the pressure and not settling for little has great benefits and is totally worth it in the long run.

Test in bits

One of the ways to reduce chances of failure and rejection and conserve your time, energy and creativity for bigger and better things is to test your ideas in bits and parts. Also, when it comes to sharing ideas with others, I have realized it's better if you do so in bits.

This means that if your idea has say 6 parts then each of the 6 parts you'll share with different people according to their expertise or based on your relationship with them or the trust you have in them.

This way you will be able to prevent the idea from being copied or "stolen" as society calls it. (When it is the society that steals in different ways, different things which are very wrong and unethical.)

The method shared above will also give you a solid foundation for each part as each part will be given due time and expertise and not overburden any one person with the whole idea.

Imagine the worst and best that can happen

For any person or organization, in whatever interaction or dealing you have, think of what's the best thing that can happen when you are with this organization or person? Now think of the worst thing that can happen when you are with this person or organization?

So let's say for a certain proposal, the boy and family, income and lifestyle, character and manners were good and they were in the west. What's the best thing that could happen? I'd have a great luxurious life and afford the latest things I wanted, my parents would be happy.

Now, what's the worst thing that can happen? All that I learned and built myself for, was for India and geography-specific first and then global. I'd have to change all that in my goals and leave the country that gave me everything and made me who I am. I would serve another country with the best I received from the best globally. I knew I would feel guilty all my life for being a loser, an escapist, a person who took the shortcut and settled for little.

Another example was of a "great and educated" boy and family, with a science background and common hometown, my parents were happy.

What's the worst thing that could happen? I wouldn't be "allowed" to work or study and that my resume was too much. I told myself: "Madiha, your parents invested in your education, God blessed you with such talents, are you going to let you down and let God down?"

Think of an organization or a company with almost everything a person who wanted to work in the social sector would want. What's the best thing that could happen? Great job, great position and fame, salary and opportunities to travel and network.

What's the worst thing that could happen? I would lose my freedom, I would have to follow orders and create policies and plans that would prick my conscience and it may not be good for humanity at large or my nation more specifically and that at this early phase of my career, I may not have the maturity to deal with effectively and end up with a lose-lose situation for myself and project/task as well as for the different people or sides concerned.

Now after reflecting on the best and worst things that can happen, you can take calculated risks for your study, work, career, cause or relationships. Don't let society, your loved ones or peers influence your decision as the majority of them might focus on success and failure over a period of their lifetime or yours and for their immediate family and community.

You must think big when it comes to taking risks (calculated ones) and the impact they would have in the next decade or why not a century to come and not only on yourself, your immediate and present family and your country.

Think about what's the best thing that can happen if you took the risk- to yourself, humanity, country, community and family?

Now think about the worst thing that could happen if you took the risk- to yourself, humanity, country, community and family.

The order may vary depending on different situations.

Here I am referring to the family being sad or hurt when let's say you said yes to a path that you created or followed that will help you serve humanity better.

Backup Plans

On one hand, society teaches you to have a fixed focus and goals and not bend while on the other hand, it preaches you to go with the flow. I always had great confusion on this subject but I'm learning and will continue to do so.

However, in the last few years of my life, when I started from scratch, when I started building myself and my empire, I learned that it's good to have backup plans and if due to any unavoidable circumstances you couldn't make them ahead of time then at least have a mindset and attitude to do it. That will prevent you from being depressed and save a lot of time.

Sometimes you might end up making spontaneous plans too as things feel right and things work out for better and more impact.

So for example when I didn't get the college of my dreams, I had my mother who advised me to apply to a college that didn't have my subject. I was willing to explore and didn't want to waste a year. I didn't want to study in the other college where I didn't follow the language and had lesser activities.

I knew what I wanted and what I didn't want (not the complete list but yes partial) and I took the dive. I used my backup plan and this college was not the college of my dreams but turned out to be the college for my dreams.

This is where I met my most trusted teacher and mentor, Professor Dr. Illora Sen where I started cricket for the first time as an official tournament in a girl's college in my city.

This is where I developed the confidence, courage and character to do the work I'm doing today.

I learned to lead and be actively involved with seniors and juniors, teaching and domestic staff, academics and sports, public speaking and singing, planning and hosting events.

What you or society may consider as rejection and failure could really be a redirection by God and for your dreams, for the person you always wanted to be and you didn't know or maybe you knew you were meant to be.

It could also be that when God sees you are not fulfilling your potential or purpose, he may send the signs or make things happen or send people or events that will act as Catalyst to help you. I believe this happens when your intentions are good, when you are constantly seeking and striving to improve yourself and the world around you.

REFLECT:

1. What kind of rejections have you faced in life? How did you deal with them? How did you feel after being "rejected" by them?

2. What action will you take after reading this chapter on "Inspiration 2" to deal with failure and rejection in your life? Think about how you would deal with it and how would you advise someone who has gone through the failure and rejection you faced.

III

It is Written so it will happen vs Work hard and make it happen?

Due to past failures and rejection, a lot of people mess up their present and future, believing that a bad past = bad present = bad future. This could be due to lack of motivation or society's pressure but more than that it's due to a lack of purpose in life or the purpose and focus been shaken up due to challenges and struggles from outside or inside.

Bad past leads to bad future?

Bad experiences and failures in the past may lead you to believe that you will have a bad future and thus fill your heart and mind with fear. That is the case with a lot of elders in the society where due to their circumstances in their past if they failed or couldn't achieve something or due to their present regret or guilt or failure may result in them making you believe the same.

It certainly isn't easy to live the life of your dreams, to be the woman or man of your dreams but it's totally worth it.

Believe me it will get easier along the way if only you start. Miracles will come if you believe and work for them.

So how do you change the equation of bad past to bad future and make it bad past to great future?

It won't happen through only wishing, only praying, only hard work and grind, only good intentions, only learning every day. You will get the results you want when you do all of these and daily.

The equation and ultimately your life will change, your present and future will be great when you change your habits and your daily rituals, when you change your mindset, when you take control of yourself, your thoughts and feelings and only sometimes allow them to overwhelm, overpower or dominate you. Over time you would be mastering them.

It wasn't easy and it isn't easy for me even now after saying yes to myself and my dreams but I'm going to keep striving to evolve and get better. I'm sure that as I evolve and get better so will the world.

Changing mindset, the thought process and the systems may take time but you have to be a quick learner and prioritise it, give it time and energy, be willing to ask, answer and apply in your daily life and not preach it simply.

It's very important to have clarity in life and to have a sense of purpose even if it's not crystal clear about the "what." The "why" must be very clear and "how" getting clearer as you work after you have started the journey.

In to out and out to in

The changes that take place internally will be reflected externally and the reverse is also true that the changes that take place externally will be reflected internally but there has to be a balance and a mechanism to deal with both.

If a calamity, a tragedy, artificial or man-made occurs and that is external then your mood, your thoughts, your life and lifestyle- everything might undergo a huge change and that change is internal.

When there were arguments in the family or with the family about my study, work, dreams, marriage, a lot of times I was so overwhelmed that for hours I was unable to focus, in spite of selecting battles wisely and not reply to everything told to me. I was unable to act according to my schedule or to-do list for that day.

I am now able to overcome the negativity in a shorter period of time. I try listening to motivational music and talks and if I'm angry then I workout simultaneously to get the negative energy channelised in a better way. I make weekly goals and stay up at night on some other days after the incident has occurred to finish the work.

I fight the mind battle. With my own mind.

Giving up isn't an option and I tell myself:

"Madiha, you must always remember how your actions today will help you have that great future you deserve. You must have it because you invested in yourself and have come so far. How can you quit!"

This will be a daily affair where the inside affects the outside and the outside affects the inside.

A very important thing to note here is that after watching or reading about sad, depressing, hopeless daily news, you must not allow yourself to be affected so much that your present state and focus gets affected and you can't work productively.

By all means feel sad, upset and even angry but tell yourself that that energy and time needs to be utilised more for building something positive that will also be a solution to solve that problem, incidents or tragedies that have occurred and that bother you.

Every day, you'll come across people wanting and needing your help in a small or big way. Helping is great but your bigger goal, vision and mission must not be shifted or distracted as a result of your time and energy gone in helping everyone too much daily.

I learnt to either delegate that to my peers, juniors, seniors, people or organisation that I knew or sometimes just pray or offer words of encouragement. It wasn't possible to help everyone, every time.

I recall a lady at a wedding who was the mother of my ex-student asking for help for herself and her daughters education and I told her briefly what she could do because she was quick and smart to be able to figure out but she kept pushing me for my number and help. Another time, a girl contacted me on Facebook for career advice and then messaged on whatsapp telling me once that I did what I loved and she wanted to do too and another time she told me that her uncle "knew" me and suggested her to contact me. On asking who he was, I realised that he was into social work and very rarely liked or commented. I didn't "know" him.

A friend once called up to say she wanted to help a woman who was going through mental trauma, family conflict and police case but she didn't know the whole story and had little time to help. I told her: "I have a big dream and goal to achieve and if I put my energy, time, thought and creativity into it then all the smaller problems won't happen so frequently. I will choose to focus on the big goal along with helping in limits each day in smaller ways because I have my own challenges too. I need to invest my hours well and at this stage be a bit "money-minded" and "choosy" so that my efforts and focus remain on track otherwise I'll end up being dependent on others for financial needs and that will reduce my freedom. I will not be able to publish my book, build the dream organisations and projects or be the woman of my dreams who will empower others and then raise an empowered generations to come."

Take one day at a time for improving yourself. It's important to have life goals for every phase and have a to-do list, clear vision and mission. It's important that you strive to make your today better than yesterday and your tomorrow better than today. I follow the 3 R's theory- Reduce, Replace and Reflect, which I observed in my life through different experiences that helped to reduce guilt and fear in my life.

The outside will not change if the inside doesn't change.

Society wants the outside world to change and then individuals to change.

That's not my way.

I believe that individuals must change first and then society and the world will change.

Society expects girls to do and be a certain way. Most of these expectations seemed meaningless to me because those who emphasised a lot on them were into family politics, had no focus in life, for them only cooking and cleaning, maids working, going and coming by car, wearing good branded clothes, obeying orders and controlling others, fame and what will people say, good furniture and utensils, just reading holy book, calling up maulana or pundits for solving small problems, emotional blackmail were daily things and important too.

I didn't want to be average like these folks because I had greater responsibility and bigger dreams. I stopped listening to others stories and politics they played in their houses or life. I stopped taking sides when in the past that was such an important battle and my voice the loudest.

I stopped spending time worrying or focusing or listening on how today's generation doesn't want to listen or how arrogant I had become that I didn't listen to anyone especially elderly, that after years of sacrifice, hard work and love, I was not grateful, obedient, willing to compromise. I started to invest in my brother and in my cousin sister and taught both at the same time when earlier they had fights but they learnt to study together.

I started to encourage my aunt, uncle and cousin brother too. I started becoming more understanding of mom and dad, their individual personalities and relationship with each other and stopped taking sides but joked rarely and defended one before the other. I started giving better explanations to problems to my grandparents that made them respect my work time and privacy at home and that made my grandma (who was married in her teens and never studied further than primary school) say: "If there were more people (maras meaning man as well as men) like Madiha then the world will surely change for the better," and that made my grandfather say: "Earlier people knew you as my granddaughter but now people tell me as your grandfather. I get more respect from such and such leader because of your work."

That made my youngest sister say: "Now that sister of ours has learnt to speak up more when earlier she would not."

That made my 9 year old brother once say: "A person should study first then work and fulfill their dreams and then get married and have babies."

That made my dad (whom society called conservative) say: "I have left you to God. He will take care of you," and he stood up for me on several occasions.

That made my mother say in my absence: "If Madiha was there she would say that the beetroot red colour in the juice is so strong that it will not let other colours dominate."

These changes happened when I took the initiative, when I said yes to me and my dreams and to becoming the woman of my dreams.

At the same time, I started changing lives of people outside- where I got calls and messages saying: "When you speak, you make us believe." or "You look and sound like us but you are giving us hope that if you can do it so can we." or "You are working so slowly, steadily and peacefully. Keep it up." or "You are the pride for this community."

I stopped preaching and started living my message as much as possible.

I continue to strive to make my life my message to the world so that there is more impact, more credibility, more people relating to me and I can relate to them, so that God sends miracles my way and helps me create legacy that is big and deep.

History doesn't need to repeat itself

I recall reading in school that history repeats itself and most people allow that belief to rule their life, their habits and mindset.

No wonder it repeats for them.

History was my favourite subject at school. History is about stories- stories of people, of people who impacted other people. Change will not come by repeating history or by complaining.

Change will come when history is changed. What happened years ago is history today. After many years, today will be history too. Changing history required to change stories and if today's stories are changed then history will change.

I told myself at 23:

"How can I change stories of millions of people. That's difficult and impossible for me. I can't change so many stories but yes I can change my story and if I change my story then the world will know a new story. Enough is enough. Enough of blame game. That must stop."

I didn't want to be that adult who would say: "The world is like that. This is how it has always been."

I didn't want to be a woman spending all day worrying on what to cook and serve, clean, fight and argue with family-parents, in laws, spouse and kids, neighbours and relatives.

I didn't want to be like those women who spent time at gym talking of other women, people and where they would hangout out or seek entertainment or like those at the airport busy on their phones discussing what they would buy from online shops.

I didn't want to be a social worker who is known for posing for photographs, speaking at every event and on every cause, attending parties and sounding "polished," "intellectual," "foreign," "always speaking," "among elites only." I didn't want these to be an important part of my life.

I didn't want to be the young person whose important hours of life were full of parties and socialising, purposeless work, volunteering or study and who would go with the flow, who would be a problem creator by being into unethical and unproductive activities, who fell in love for the sake of it, married for the sake of it.

I didn't want to be average. Average was boring to me and that was not going to be me. I had told myself again and again.

I didn't want to be like the rest but help them by leading them to be the best.

Here are a few lessons I learnt based on my life:

Identify what is it in your life, your family, your society, country or world that you don't want to be repeated? Analyse why you don't want it to repeat?

What gain will it bring to humanity? What pain will it reduce for humanity?

Research, build, learn, collaborate with others to deal with it and to change it by reducing the pain or increasing the gain for humanity.

Take wisdom and lessons from the great people of the past, who went through great struggles to become great by making the people and world around them great, by contributing by being an asset to humanity, by being the winds of change.

Select what practices will help you from their life and whether application must be direct or with modifications to suit your case and context.

Learn from the best of the past and apply in your life and reject the worst of the past and create a better present and future that will bring you peace, satisfaction and happiness and to millions in the world.

Keep striving to be an asset to humanity and creating a better and more ethical world than the one you grew up in even if that means to challenge and reject ethics set up by culture or meaningless people-pleasing concepts and ideologies. The journey and outcome will be worth it.

Start

Bad experiences of the past, shortage of resources or knowledge in the present, fear and uncertainty of the future might prevent you from starting on your dreams and your journey of becoming the person of your dreams.

When I started in March 2016, I started from scratch- zero contacts, zero resources and zero organisation connects. I had given up and abandoned and resigned from everything.

I was in great depression with all hope gone from humanity, at times wishing for death because I saw no purpose in life but the heart sought Him. I was in prostration sometimes and sometimes looking at the sky, sometimes hands raised in prayer and sometimes wiping tears.

I felt like I had nowhere to go, no path or guidance, no one to trust but Him. My state was such that my present and future seemed uncertain and all the frustration, anger, hurt and betrayal built up.

But I just started.

I read Quran and underlined words that gave me hope like the verse talking of the whole world coming together wanting to hurt or benefit you then it wouldn't be able to, unless God willed it, on good men for good women and good women for good men, verses on young men of the cave or on miracles.

I read books and stuck sticky notes with my insights, reflections and action tips to help me like "Promise of a Pencil" by Adam Braun, "Three cups of Tea" by Greg Mortenson and David Oliver Relin, "Unbreakable" by Mary Kom, "Ignited Minds" by Dr.A.P.J Abdul Kalam.

I gazed at the sky when it was raining or late at night, sharing with Him my pain and struggles, fears and possibilities. I knew He was listening and the only One who understood and still does.

I felt and believed that when He sees that I'm doing my best with good intentions and hard work, He will send miracles my way. I wanted to earn before anything else to start being financially independent and making my own choices and decisions on how and where to spend my money. Or pay at least 1 bill of general household expenses to show that my money is ours too. I then wanted to learn to increase my knowledge and skill set to have a better future for myself and the world and serve humanity better.

a) Earning

Start earning if you are not. Your parents may be rich, supporting you, your education and interests but for how long and why?

Society will suggest marry a rich person and you won't have to worry about hard work to earn and your needs will be completely taken care of. I learnt from my own life that financial independence makes you strong, gives you a voice, makes people look up and listen to you, to allow you to make your own choices.

It is important to earn.

In the first few years, doing dream work and especially doing it full time and having dream salary may be difficult, not impossible though. It wasn't easy for me atleast. This is how I figured out.

I looked up from my own family and relatives list, teachers and trusted elders list, what earning and learning opportunities I could get. I had limitations of not being able to work outside home for long hours then but I wanted a salary to be independent to fulfill my basic needs to start with.

I applied at Lifebushido and my recruit process in Triangles was a unique experience and after sharing my story, my boss Steve Kantor sent an email saying he looked forward to working with me.

God was at work and planning, sending miracles.

My salary wasn't much in the first few months but that was the beginning of what economic independence does and means in a person's life and especially in the life of a young woman. I got to learn from people very different from me and who made different and similar choices. I got more time to learn karate, to volunteer and explore what I wanted to do ahead in life. I was proud to introduce myself and share about my work and observe the "wow" expression when I said a virtual US based company and got more respect from those who thought I was average all along. At the same time, I was looking for opportunities locally or nationally and work from home again as I wasn't sure if I'd get "permission" to go out and work, if my body was ready for it yet and my soul ready for this battle to convince others when it was so hard to fight my internal battles.

I decided to go slow and learn the work.

I kept seeking opportunities but most of them didn't make sense in spite of reading and applying. I'm glad they didn't work out.

I had my own mind, my way of working, my creativity and I was good at several things so either the job would bore me or I would be too much for them to steal their ideas or I asked too many questions. Sometimes I didn't say yes because it meant good pay but may be I would not be able to do what's good for my country first but for others interests.

I decided to invest more time in what I was good at- writing and speaking, building my social enterprise YouEd to empower others to lead, who may be going through similar challenges like teens, youth, women in particular and I would be open to employing men too.

My book, content writing, teaching and public speaking is what I was depending on for being financially independent and sustain my causes, projects and lifestyle and to be able to contribute to family expenses no matter how small.

b) Learning

When I finished my high school where I studied pure science, I applied for Bachelors in Zoology but landed with Botany for which I'm very grateful to God and my mom. I would have got bored with zoology.

After bachelor's, a lot of people including family and teachers insisted that I do a B.Ed or TTC but I didn't want to for the sake of a degree. Ladies in the gym would also say: "You should have done or should do your masters." (Assuming that I'd do in Botany related fields.)

I told them: "I don't want to follow the traditional path of doing a bachelors and then masters and PhD for the sake of it. It's my investment- with time, money and effort. Taking a break and exploring opportunities will give me clarity into what are the best options and prospects for the future."

Most people thought I was wasting time and acting crazy and that I would regret this one day but this didn't happen because very recently I came across people who took a break after bachelors.

I felt strange but again I was seeing God at work.

This was the tribe He wanted me to have and He was sending them in my life. They were like-minded, had made or were making similar choices while going through similar struggles.

I completed my bachelor's in 2014 and till early 2018, I indulged in self-learning through articles videos and courses online. I took +Acumen courses on social entrepreneurship, storytelling for change, networking leadership, lean data and lean startup, adaptive leadership, human-centered design and design kit and access to capital for women. I learnt about digital marketing from digital garage, moodle from learn moodle and while doing these I learnt to use Zoom, Wiziq, NovoEd platforms that got me interested in technology more and using it to empower others through education and economic independence.

I watched a lot of TEDx talks on various subjects that helped me think inside the box, outside the box and thinking there is no box. I learnt through the OpenIDEO challenges to collaborate, to build ideas and connect ideas, to meet incredible changemakers like Isaac Jumba from Kenya and Kate Rushton from United Kingdom who I'm still friends with.

On +Acumen, I met my family of global changemakers and lovely people from the team of +Acumen like Marica, Amy, Joshua and others. I'm grateful to all of them for their encouragement and appreciation especially after my TEDx.

The 3-4 years of self-learning and self-discovery made me realise I wanted to learn about journalism and mass communication, public administration, adult learning, human psychology, educational leadership and some others. These topics would equip me to lead better in the years to come along with self-learning through different websites and different means of learning like workshops, seminars, books, webinars, articles, events in my field or related fields as it helps me to improve my knowledge, meet like minded people.

I continue to learn about communication techniques, strategy, content development, marketing, organisation, presentation, networking as they help me to improve these existing skills in me and gives me ideas to improve my work and cause across all domains.

I had no specific goals for learning and I didn't plan ahead of time initially. As and when I came across courses, I decided to give it a shot with learning outcomes listed on the homepage.

As I did the courses, I was getting ideas on how I can implement the learning in real life. Only recently due to different activities I've been part of and the people I had been meeting, I saw more success and opportunities coming my way. That helped me figure out what I wanted to learn further.

I need to upgrade my skills and knowledge as I feel outdated very quickly.

I needed more learning in the years to come to help me grow personally and professionally, to equip myself to lead better in the educational and social sector and for all my dream work and projects.

More than anything, learning gave me confidence, made me humble, made me contribute and add valuable insights for personal and professional growth for myself and others.

Learning and Doing helps me to be an asset to my country and humanity.

Journey and Destination

The struggles of life and those in the world often make me think about my life's purpose.

When I was upset, depressed, hopeless, lacking any resources at 23, I used to rarely but yet feel: "This is the end of it. I can't take it anymore. There are way too many struggles and I'm not so strong. I'm tired of battles and challenges every day. I wish my life ended."

I didn't give up though, there was a soft voice that kept telling me: "There is more than what your loved ones and society are talking about. You don't have to be like them. Majority kept living in a fantasy world where everything is ideal but fake and full of deceit. Majority encourage pretense-families and couples to be happy when they may be hating each other. They show and act as if everything is right and good when it really may be terrible, be it situation or relationship. They show mother and daughter or mother in law and daughter in law relationships to be perfect when either or both must be going through mental torture due to the other. They say "how lovely" or "I'm so happy" but in reality they may be thinking and feeling: "I wish you are never happy because I never got it or I don't have it." They have their own set path for a girl and a separate or sometimes a similar one for a boy. They want every person to live a set path and follow the same rules, do and say the same things irrespective of what the individuals want or aspire for. They want a girl or a boy to be like a product from the factory or market, all made similar and in bulk (when it is they only who object to "objectifying" women.) They wouldn't allow her to work at a factory or the market to study, work or to improve it."

According to society, marriage is the ultimate for which a boy or especially a girl "should" learn, work, dress, speak, act, live and make choices in a certain way to be successful, to attract a good match and then follow more typical norms.

Elders often want history to repeat as they say: "It was like this and this in our times. It has to be done this way. No one has ever protested or objected as elders advise and obedience is more important. Today's generation is so spoilt. They won't listen even."

They want that what happened to them, what they did and how they did should repeat with their children and grandchildren, failing to realise that change takes place every minute, every hour, every day and every month, every year.

Change will take place in every decade and with every generation, the challenges and therefore the way of life and your attitude towards it has to be modified, choices they make, how they make and the outcomes will vary if the core principles and values are derived and preserved keeping in mind the greater good for humanity and for yourself.

For me, life is a journey from the time you are born till the time you leave this world and even afterward as I believe in life after death where the ultimate decision and your eternal fate is decided. I believe that there are only two fates in the after life- you are of the good or evil and then your forever journey of the life of eternal pleasure and happiness starts or your forever journey of eternal misery and unhappiness starts.

The concept of destination in my life is pertaining to paradise or hell as the ultimate destination for which I must work hard and strive all my life until I die. I believe that due to corruption in this world and us being human beings, we can't always do justice, not even judges (like in my brother's kidnapping case.)

That people who are mistreated are not always given their due and justice. That those who sacrifice for noble causes and with noble intentions are not always rewarded, that those who have toiled all their life, undergone pain and suffering and then die, have never seen comfort and got reward they deserved. That those who die early or lose their loved ones don't get to spend time with them.

Hereafter is the place where everything will fall into place what couldn't be in this world. Justice will be given by God and every soul shall get what it deserves based on what the soul has strived for and chosen.

Whenever people ask me my present state, I try to say that "I'm striving" to do such and such things or "I'm on the journey" towards this and this and there are expectations when I don't say the above. The reason I use the above phrases is because it's not the end.

Becoming a bachelors, masters or PhD, becoming a spouse or parent or grandparent, becoming a leader and holding a position is not the end.

It is rather the beginning of a journey that will need lots of investment in terms of knowledge, time, efforts and intentions.

The above mindset helps me to keep striving, growing and evolving for the better, it gives me a balance in life and between pride and humility, most importantly to become the woman of my dreams who will strive for justice and peace, who will be an asset to mankind and leave behind a legacy.

REFLECT:

1. What are the different incidents and events from the past that you think are not letting you work now or for your future? Write down the incidents in brief and the fears or concerns associated with it.

2. What action will you take after reading this chapter on "Inspiration 3" to deal with your fears and insecurities about the present and the future?

IV

Successful like the majority or the minority?

Everyone wants success but not everyone understands its true meaning.

Society has terribly failed to create a successful majority- when it is with pride that it claims to have done so- bulk production of identical souls that are in misery, purposeless and lost, confused and distracted, wasting resources and following society's same map for all.

This is not success but failure on society's part. This leads to so much pain and suffering in the world and humanity.

Here are my insights, reflections and inspirations on success and impact:

Redefining success

At 23, I realized what society kept calling as success and still does is to get married to a "good man" and in a "good family," have "good life" and "good income."

In addition to these, she must have "skills" to compromise and to keep quiet in the face of injustice, when unjust words are uttered or unjust actions are done by people of greater power, age and resources.

I didn't want to be average so I started thinking of other not so average people, the minority population, who created a legacy and left behind a legacy.

I realized success for me was the attainment of one goal or conquering and climbing one mountain and embarking on the next goal or mountain simultaneously or on the completion of one.

Success to me was the sense of satisfaction and happiness I got during the process, the lives I touched, the greater insight I developed to help me improve my personal and professional life and of others.

Success to me is when I can connect peacefully to God and the nature He created without guilt and to be able to admit my mistakes before Him, seek His forgiveness, to talk to Him (in prostration or looking at the sky or silently in my heart or as a prayer) daily and sometimes after a break of forgetfulness on my part but my heart telling me to seek Him.

Success to me is when I'm able to judge myself or others but very soon able to and willing to give others a chance, to understand them, to pray for them and if I don't see positive results then to carry on and work on and with people, in whom I see more potential and scope for growth and when I see growth in me.

Success to me is when I am able to surrender to God, to fight my own mind battle and heart battle and not with people or society. It is when I give in to fighting the internal conflict and chatter-box and then have the ability to look at the world around differently and finding solutions to the problems and suffering of the world.

Process and Products, Quality and Quantity

Process and Product

In the past several years, I thought that success is more about the process than the product but of course the product counts and it's important to keep it in mind.

In the last 5-6 years, I've done a lot of different things and the product is me but I had not been able to develop or be something concrete, crisp and clear as society likes it or even as I would have liked it until several months ago.

Here are some of my reflections based on my observations and experiences on process and product:

-The process really matters to ensure that the path taken and the means adopted to achieve something, is ethical and transparent, as dishonest means will affect the impact in the long term. For example, most of the students in my school and college were more focused on getting the first division and being top scorers in exams and get a good degree with good marks.

I had never really thought of cheating until the third year due to my illness, I wasn't prepared. The curriculum and exams format is outdated and boring. I had to cheat otherwise I would not even pass. I was wrong in doing that.

That incident makes me think of how superficial success is and is based on what our society and environment have drilled in us. Majority of the students don't even think of it and most parents have no problem with cheating as their chest will be filled with pride and head held high if their children do well.

Everyone considers this as part of growing up, being young and having fun, enjoying college and life, creating memories. I truly believe that if the focus is on the process then the chances of dishonesty and corruption are reduced.

-The process is also important because in case the product or outcome is not what you expected or imagined then at least the investment made in the process yields good results. It did in my case.

Today I'm neither studying or working in the field directly or closely related to the subject I did my bachelors in- botany. I however invested in those 5 years- 2 in high school and 3 in college and that helps me till today. I learned about scientific thinking, logical reasoning, replicability, standardization, giving things a structure and order, connecting things, measuring input and output, cause and effect, great observation skills, framing good questions and asking them, striving for accurate results at the end of experiments or processes.

-The product is equally important as I realized after meeting my soul tribe members and learning about life.

In my case, I had no role models for the work I wanted to do or the person I wanted to be.

I often felt lost in the beginning as I had no one to tell me what to do and how to do or even why to do it. I am the eldest granddaughter and daughter. Society and the elders often spoke of marriage and typical average talks so it never struck me for years to think about my life's purpose and have life goals.

I am grateful to God for all these experiences as my journey taught me what I would have never discovered otherwise as an average. He sent people to guide me so that I may now guide and inspire others to not be average, to help them realize their life's purpose.

-The focus on the product gives you a clarity of purpose in life and how you are going to fulfill that purpose, what problems you are going to solve in the world and what legacy you'll leave behind in this world and be known for?

-Success lies in the balance between process and product.

One of the ways to maintain that balance is to have clear aims, outcomes and ways to measure impact for whatever you do. Get that on paper before you start. Maintain a diary or journal. The product could be monetary gain, recognition, award, changing lives, feeling good and content with life, people using what products and services you provide and how they benefit from it.

Now, in the last few years, I have started to get that balance due to my mentors, soul tribe members and friends.

Quality and Quantity

My mom would often tell me out of concern to focus on quality over quantity as she saw that most people around me and people of my age were running after quantity. An example is that most people want a lot of money and they may often forget about how they earn it. Most people may want one degree after another for the sake of it or just for fame more than gaining knowledge and skills that they would achieve.

I didn't want to be like that.

Yes, there are great examples of people who didn't do well academically but achieved a lot because they had the skill set that the education system failed to impart and they had developed skills on their own and practiced self-learning.

I wanted a good income (quantity) but not just through any job or work. I would do what makes me happy and satisfied, helps me improve, to acquire new skills and give back to society with a cause at its core.

Living a simple life and living a life in poverty are two different things and I do believe in simplicity and minimalism moderately and in many aspects of my life but poverty is something I'm fighting to reduce or remove.

Poverty causes many problems as does wealth. I have seen examples of wealthy people with brains that feel and hearts that think. I have also seen examples of wealthy, selfish and greedy people who waste resources and are unkind.

I want to be like the former.

Being a multipotentialite and multi-talented in school, I've learned to do several things and not to restrict myself and my impact. At school and college, I was an all-rounder, studying hard, playing sports, participating in extracurricular activities, enjoying taking initiatives and leadership roles, spending time learning from teachers, juniors, seniors and peers and trying to create an impact. After passing out of college, I did teach and work for 1-2 organizations but that did not yield results that I wanted. I was too attached to the organization and when things went wrong and I was too hurt, I didn't want to be associated with anyone from those organizations anymore.

I realized the need for doing something of my own as well as working for an organization as that would help me grow personally and professionally, financially and spiritually, mentally and creating social impact.

At 23, I realized that I was a multipotentialite by nature as the characteristics became more prominent.

I wanted to learn more, do more and be more.

I took up a lot on my plate and very often struggled with time management and stress due to lack of sleep and being always busy.

Once while discussing with my close friends I could put the pieces together and connect all my passions, interests and roles and during the conversation the explanation that I gave- how would I do and why I must do it, I got the clarity and answers.

Over time, I started realizing the need to develop expertise in my domains of work and acquire more knowledge and skills through certified or even non-certified courses to build my resume, to be academically and professionally stronger for myself and serving humanity.

I learned to do multiple things and play multiple roles.

People kept criticising me for doing too much, for having no focus and a single goal. They saw me struggle but very few people among my mentors and soul tribe understood me. Naziha is a mentor who was introduced by Steve from Lifebushido, gave me a wonderful advice that I could do multiple things if that made me happy and if I was able to do them and when it gets overwhelming, I could take a step back or delegate. My close friends also listen to my explanation, continue to support and give feedback. Pallavi, an RJ who I met during the Women Leadership Summit in Kolkata also encouraged me and assured that it was okay to be a multipotentialite.

That made me strive harder to come up with a schedule and "algorithm" for my life and goals.

I would keep improving it and still do what feels right after discussion and practice and as changes occur every day in the environment and therefore even in me so I try to make the most of the resources, opportunities and to be able to meet the needs of humanity and my country better and mine too.

When I want to do too many things and my quality starts to get compromised, I create a timeline and focus on one or few things more than the rest and either delegate or use the current projects to build others to come later on- to gather research, resources or revenue or networks for them.

I understood that Delegation and Collaboration works well with Multipotentialites like me. We can do more and at the same time develop expertise in all the domains while creating impact. That saves time, energy, resources and more can be accomplished in less time.

Inner and Outer Success, Hidden and Apparent Success

Majority of the world is after outer success and success that is apparent. I, however, feel that being truly successful means to have success that is inside and outside, which is hidden and apparent. All four types are equally important and will add to the impact you are striving to make.

Success according to me is when while striving to make a difference and change the world, I grow as a person, I become better and my character develops. Success is when I continue to fight against my inner struggles, bad habits and traits and seek to improve myself. My greatest struggles and therefore greatest success so far has been in investing in myself, to have started changing myself for the better, to focus on me and building a better me to serve humanity and contribute to a better society, country and the world.

Too often people focus on the outside like I saw most people in the world do it and those in my family and immediate circles focus on the inside mostly. I didn't like the imbalance and conflicts that arose as a result of either extreme attitude. I decided I'll strive to achieve that balance and to prove to myself what I could do and what was important. To improve myself, I started cutting out on the entertainment time and methods and means that I used earlier. There were and are times when I'm tempted to watch serials and movies and shows which were popular and fun but I realized I couldn't afford distractions or unproductive thoughts or spend time on something that was unproductive, that would not lead to positive growth.

I watched selective things and that too skipping parts if there was more entertainment in it or if I got the gist or if there was too much drama or negativity. I cut down on parties and social gatherings, hanging out time in spite of being an extrovert and known among people. I knew it would serve as a distraction in many ways- elders talk of marriage or start family politics or talk of maid or staff and they are bad, spending time on unnecessary activities and wasting resources. I couldn't afford that fun and popularity otherwise I would go off track at a time when I was trying to figure out the choices and path I must take to be the woman of my dreams. Now, I attend certain parties and social gatherings either because the cause is close to my heart and part of my work domain or it is related to a subject of my interest or to network productively or for the people I loved or looked upto. Weddings I have started to avoid or make visits shorter as the relatives and elders asked too many unnecessary questions and sometimes disturb my peace of mind and focus. Their typical talk was so boring, irritating and distracting when it influenced my immediate folks.

I feel a sense of achievement and success when I do my best each day and go to sleep in peace with the determination to do better the next day. Inner success for me is when I know why I do what I do and I don't feel the need to explain in details everything to anyone. Inner success is when I'm able to do charity at home and outside home. It is when I understand leadership at home better and leadership at work better as time passes by and as I grow. My elders would often say charity begins at home- "You are so good but look at you at home."

Some of my biggest achievements and success have been at home.

-The investment in my brother's education to see him overcome his nervousness, be a confident boy who can connect ideas, express himself and the ability to reflect and analyze things. I have seen this over 7-8 years in different ways. At school, during history period in class 3, he and his group were asked to choose a sub-topic under 19th and 21st century India. This is what Muhammad came and told me: "Aapi, I wanted to choose education or women. Most of my friends wanted education so we chose that. I wanted to do on women."

When he was kidnapped and then after 19 hours he returned, listening to his story, I felt proud. He was becoming the child I always thought was possible inspite of the education system and society and accordingly I invested in him. He showed positive results to everything I did with him and did to him. He proved my cause and belief in "stronger kids, safer world" true. His way of thinking and working, his leadership and concern for the world, his power of observation, connection and reflection- all amaze me as I feel successful to have invested in one child. I developed my own ideas and models of parenting, teaching, social change based on that and tested parts of it in an orphanage or with other kids and parents.

I've seen and felt success.

-My youngest sister is a black belt at 16 who learned karate in a co-ed environment, went to a winter camp of almost 1 week in a mixed group, participated and fought in a unisex competition. I wasn't allowed to learn karate or lawn tennis because the teacher was male. My being a Rebel with Purpose did turn things around. I'm so proud of her and my parents. I keep encouraging her to make a career out of it- part or full time and she agreed because she loves karate. I keep looking out for opportunities where she could teach and train more girls and women and boys too. I learned till blue belt from her so that by training me, someone older, she would get confidence from now. I want her to be very successful and be an achiever from an early age.

-I lived in a typical family where the fights (big and small) between the families of two brothers was common. The conversation and attempts to prove "who is better" was common. At one point in time, before turning 23, I was one of those who took sides and practiced the typical things. I stopped all that and started the "not so average" practice. I encouraged my uncle, aunt and cousins to do better. I praised them, gave them feedback out of concern and honesty, stopped the conversation if I started the fun or pulling their leg. I started teaching my cousin just so I could invest in another girl child and from my family, be there as a mentor to her. Those meaningless fights have stopped and I ignore them if ever spoken about. I often tell my elders, "There are people dying in the world, there are so many problems outside and we are stuck in all these small things. We can't think small." I take credit for this change and for the transformation that had occurred. I love it when my uncle or aunt come to me to share their success or their children's success or even weaknesses or failures as I'm earning their trust and respect too.

I intend to continue this in a bigger way when I'm married so that during that phase of my life, I can continue to be a role model. Innovation is needed in that field too. Doing so then will give me greater credibility to understand and talk on it, to reach more people and help them, to develop solutions and insights on it and create a bigger and deeper impact together with the family. I have certain projects in mind on that.

-The same father who would worry a lot about safety and door to door drop and pick up for comfort suggested for my Surat trip to receive an award to have an auto in case it gets late or it's far. He didn't stop or say no. Another time at home while I was sharing my day's events and I thought he was concerned so I tried to console. He said: "I've left you to Allah. He will take care of you." I always knew this was his real and true potential but circumstances and the critical society prevented him from doing it. This was the same man who was known to take tension for the smallest and biggest of things. I believe this change happened due to the success I've been getting, something most people didn't expect or imagined, due to the thought process I developed and that I was no longer taking sides but trying to arrive at a win-win solution at home. This change happened due to the way he saw me dealing with certain cases at home and with family when normally I could have created unnecessary conflict and fought unnecessary battles. He also saw all my posts, likes and comments, videos and articles. He saw and heard what people thought of me. That filled him with pride. One day while having dinner when I told him what I had in mind to gift him and mom, he said: "I only want you to be satisfied." I responded with: "Aww!" I was so happy to hear that.

-The same mother who would earlier call too often with lots of concerns and what to do and how, now trusted me more. Once she said: "Sorry to call and disturb you again. But could you get down in Poddar Court?" Earlier she would say that I shouldn't do certain things but things changed when I changed and when my priorities changed. Going to the library to write a book and that too in the holy month of Ramadan while fasting was unimaginable in the past. This time she called me to say: "Come here. If you go to the library for a shorter span of time, wouldn't it be good? Due to the blessings of this month, you will be more productive and successful. We are all going to be worried for you and transport will be a problem and the heavy traffic. In the past, none of us have been out till that time and for so many hours." She didn't say "for something not so important" or "don't go" but so politely and respectfully. I responded with: "Yes mom. I had that in mind too. I'm making a routine as you suggested."

I will give my best FOR INDIA and TO INDIA

All my intentions and efforts bore fruit outside too. I've seen miracles.

At 23, when I had the choice of going to the west for a good life for myself, I said no. On being asked by an aunt from the developed world why I said no in front of my mom, I said: "I was born and brought up in India, my country. This country has made me who I am today and that you and others believe in me and appreciate me by saying that I'll do better in the west and I'm suited for the west. I grew up seeing the suffering of fellow women, of men and of the people of my country in general. I saw their struggles. I offered help and advice. I felt pain and happiness for them and with them. How can I forget and move on, for me and my well-being alone? How can I give the best I have to another country? How can I leave my nation and serve another? If the west sees the best in me and I'm suited for it then I'll be that person who will bring the best of the west to my country. I'll be that trust for the west and my country."

Today, I'm the local expert for Kolkata in the Indo-US collaboration on Women in STEM Roadshow 2018 by the U.S Department of State and a project of The Ohio State University. Today, I'm the Triangle Leader working at Lifebushido to empower women in technology in the US and globally. Today, I'm a Mentor at Aspire Foundation, with offices in the UK and USA. I'm a Mentor at Global Thinkers Mentors Forum for Telemachus 2019. I'm a TeachSDGs Ambassador Cohort 3 in 2019. Today, I'm a +Acumen (USA) community member as Catalyst Coach, Corps member and Launch team member for their courses on Udemy. Today, I'm working with Junior Horlicks for their Parenting Campaign in Kolkata when I'm yet to be a Parent and working as a Parent and Youth Mentor. One mother said: "There is so much we need to learn. We thought degrees were enough but today after hearing you, we see the need to learn from a person more learned than us!"

A group of parents said: "We need to learn and grow with our children too. We can learn so much from them. So far we blamed everyone outside but now we see we are not trained. Ma'am is right that we can change the nation." One father said: "So far my wife was learning about parenting and I thought I knew it being a doctor. But after attending your talk, I want to learn more to be a better parent."

Outer success is when after my sessions, classes, talks, conversations and even during those, people have asked me deep questions or shared deep insights and deep secrets because they trust me or they think I'll give them balanced and wise advice. A counsellor for junior school from a very reputed girls school in Kolkata told me after the parenting workshop, "Parents felt safe and secured. You are easy to trust."

For my Surat trip, when I made calls from Kolkata to organize talks there, I got positive responses from different organizations like Global Shapers Surat started a Speaker series and I was the first speaker who spoke on "Being a Global Citizen and exploring the Social Sector." Human Library Surat without checking my TEDx or detailed profile and just my brief introduction and mention of the award ceremony, gave me the opportunity to speak on Creating Human Connections. Hasti who organized it said she wanted to see how this talk would turn out. One of the Rotary Clubs in Surat, on the eve of Women's Day, invited me to share the stage with Advocate Priti Joshi from Gujarat High Court as a Speaker. I spoke on how in the name of women empowerment, we are unjust to men, on how we want men to treat us as equals but want a special "gentleman" treatment from them.

Recently, while I was standing in the bus in Kolkata and two ladies entered and complained: "Why are men sitting in the ladies seat?" I said: "When it comes to rights, we want equality. I see no problem why they can't sit?" They both were silent. I saw the respect in the eyes of the men in the bus and shock. When I moved, I saw men moving and a different attitude full of respect.

During one of my workshops on storytelling, I witnessed a girl crying profusely and share her story when she said: "I never cried for all these years because I had to be strong for my mom. Now I feel light." Her father was a gangster and she and her mom had suffered a lot.

Two boys in two different events who were heartbroken shared their stories- one of them posted on Facebook where he wrote about his vision of becoming the man of his dreams and to let go off the hurt. The other boy cried a lot and shared his story in spite of being an introvert.

At the orphanage, I saw the 100+ girls confiding in me with their inner and outer struggles and so did the staff. There were times when I got to know that they acted based on my suggestion or advice because they didn't want "Madiha Aapi to be sad or to not let her down." I saw a significant change in the girls who were serious and sincere during my URead ULead classes, their pronunciation, vocabulary and confidence increase tremendously.

Today, I'm proud to say that I'm working closely with some of the best, great people who are successful at a personal and professional level to create impact locally, nationally and globally. I don't believe in getting success alone when I can increase my impact through collaboration.

I believe in rising while helping others rise and through delegation which is why I started YouEd-Empowering YOU to LEAD and I love the work I do and the roles I play.

Replicability is important to me for impact

For me, success lies in replicability.

When I was going through struggles and challenges at 23, when people suggested I give up, some female changemakers suggested that I leave home and stay in another city for study or work. Some suggested being balanced and polite. My close friends have always given me a very balanced and genuine, effective and ethical view on life and impact. I always thought to myself: "Madiha, you must do what millions can do and replicate to be successful. You alone being a success story isn't enough for a better India and better World but it is of course, important to be a better You first. You can't move to another city to study or work just because you find it difficult or hard to do in the current setup as most women will not be able to do that. They would either be dependent on the males for finance and it's going to be an expensive move, loans are not easy to get, even more difficult to pay back."

"Madiha, you cannot give in as you know what society wants is unethical and you have to be more ethical than the society you grew up in. You will be doing injustice to God, yourself, humanity and your generations to come if you give up. You must keep testing what you do, share your story and models with the world to create more heroes and heroines even if that means you'll end up being the villain for society for sometime."

I didn't give up. I'm not giving up. I'm accountable to God and myself.

I'm responsible for my actions.

Success to me would be when I face God and tell Him: "Dear God, I did everything I could with all the talents, gifts, blessings, resources you gave me to serve You and Your people."

REFLECT:

1. What are the different definitions of success you have come across? What is your definition of success? Are you working towards success?

2. What action will you take after reading this chapter on "Inspiration 4" to be more successful in life? After reading this chapter, what new insights have you developed on success and impact?

V

What it means to Stand up and Speak up?

Success isn't possible without fighting battles- internal or external or both.

Nothing great is accomplished without fighting for truth and justice with all you have.

I see people fighting battles- small and big, my own battles made me ponder on this important subject. In my own circles and surroundings, I've seen people battling cancer and other illnesses or fighting a battle with their loved ones and family, against society or with themselves or their habits and practices or behaviour.

Here are a some of my reflections on Battles:

Life is a Test

People fighting battles made me conclude that life is a test. People we love and who love us are a test.

We appear for tests daily that we may or may not be prepared for but that our soul can handle and bear if we believe that. I realized that through my past experiences and struggles. There were struggles and challenges with family, friends, relatives, teachers, colleagues and others in society.

Some of the tests were very difficult as my character was questioned and sometimes my reputation was at stake. There were a few times I wished for death due to too much pain, hurt and guilt. Each time of those few times after making the wish for death, I talked sense into me about what would be the outcome if I died? Nothing substantial.

Dying like an average person. No. No.

I wanted to be known for something big, something wonderful. "Death isn't a good idea," I told myself. I would then read books to inspire me, to fill me with the fire to light up my life and build myself to be hope for the world and make it brighter. I listened to talks and songs and watched movies initially to inspire me to think and dream big, to overcome the overwhelming feelings that were making me feel low.

There were times when I slept almost the whole day for 2-3 months because I was depressed and hurt. I couldn't face people as I didn't know how to smile when I was so sad or how to introduce myself to them. I didn't feel like talking to anyone or smile or eat or even go anywhere.

I just wanted to shut myself off from the world because I thought it will break me, hurt me, betray me. Again and again.

I thought the world was selfish and even loved ones were selfish and will pretend to care but not think beyond physical needs or think really of the long-term and think based on what society would think and want, short or long-term.

I loved my books and my pens, my bed and my room. Eventually, the lonely time and time with God paid off and I started realizing there had to be more to my life and that I was strong as I had handled tough times before. I told myself: "Madiha, God chose you to fight this battle as hundreds of girls and women, even boys and men, may be facing similar challenges across the world. Remember this quote you read somewhere: "God gives His Toughest Battles to His Strongest Soldiers.""

I told myself that I am strong. I will find a way. I will not settle for little. I am not giving up.

He believes in me and that's why He gave me this battle and chose me to fight it. I came across another quote: "You are assigned this mountain to show others it can be moved."

I knew God wanted me to create a path, a new one. He chose me to tread on the "road not taken."

He chose me to climb and conquer a certain mountain or maybe many mountains and assigned them to me so that I could help and guide the people suffering out there and show that they can be moved.

To be successful in the tests, I started preparing myself not knowing what questions would come.

During one proposal that I didn't like, I prepared my introduction in a scientific way comparing myself to Hydrogen. That helped me to start thinking creatively again. I had watched and read about personal development before writing it. I also thought about projects I could do as per the needs of the city after research. During another proposal that I said no to but then was willing to explore a second time, I started writing my FISHES goals, listed what was same and different between me and the man and the families. That helped me understand what I was looking for in my spouse to be.

FISHES stands for Family, Intellect, Social, Health, Economic and Spiritual goals. I also thought about the projects I could do in that city. This time I felt more confident and the scope and impact of my projects were getting bigger, planning better and vision clearer. It didn't work out. Thank God! In these two cases, I was not too eager but my family was elated. They wanted me to explore without pushing me. For their happiness, I did explore but deep down I was not happy.

God knew that and that's why He played His part. He heard my prayers which is why now I strongly believe that intentions really matter because after putting in the efforts when you don't have influence then He takes over. In another proposal, I figured out what principles I was looking for and the concept of purpose, impact and legacy in me and the man I would marry. In another, I learned more about what I didn't want and what my dream was. Each of these four proposals gave me deep insights and I was not fully content to say yes and that is why I'm grateful to God that He took my side and turned them into no from the other side too.

I knew why I was doing or wanting that.

I knew that all these people would offer me great luxury and "great life" but I would be restricted professionally and personally because of their beliefs or major differences in the way I looked at life and legacy and the way they did. These were all good people and I pray God blesses them with happiness and may God guide them but my vision and mission were not aligned with theirs.

I got a big break. (phew!) I joined the gym and yoga classes, I felt something was wrong with me. I had some health challenges. I disliked talking to anyone in the gym or to my folks who accompanied me.

I focused on work out, on praying for the first few months and then started listening to music on a very simple phone. I read books to keep me engaged and watched movies or listened to music to prevent people from interacting with me. I spent those days and weeks and months in learning through videos, articles and books, even a few free courses.

I wanted to learn to grow and to come out of this state of misery and hopelessness, to be able to attract better opportunities my way. OpenIDEO and +Acumen played a big role in my growth for almost a year. I prepared for life's tests through learning. I took the social entrepreneurship 101 course with three other women, did courses on storytelling for change and networking leadership on my own. Social entrepreneurship course helped me to start figuring out what field I wanted to work in, education primarily. Storytelling for Change made me confident about my identity through a video assignment called, "Yes! I'm an Indian, a Woman, a Muslim." I was facing challenges with these three for years. On tweeting it, Greta Cowen who was the coach replied saying I'd be a good storyteller and +Acumen retweeted my video. She was right! I acquired new skills and knowledge to talk about my struggles and make it a story of strength rather than weakness.

Through networking leadership, I was able to figure out which networks and resources I could tap into and how to network, connect and expand the impact. I then did courses on Human Centered Design Thinking where I learned to empathize to solve a problem. I learned to see the problem from the other side of those I would serve. It was at this time that I met Karen, my friend with whom I was sometimes planning YouEd. We did Lean Data and Lean Strategy courses together with others. That helped us to understand how to collect data and measure impact. I did the Adaptive Leadership course where I learned how to adapt myself as a leader in different situations but stay true to myself and God. I learned about values and principles and holding on to them. I also did Systems Practice course where I felt I was finding it hard to understand some problems in the society especially the way some women treated me at the orphanage where I was volunteering.

I was surprised that I no longer blamed them but rather analyzed myself and how I could have done better. I didn't want to fight or argue or answer back as I would be wasting my precious energy and effort, time and resources. I knew the battle was not worth fighting so I critically analyzed my approach and attitude.

I realized I wanted to lead by example and not be a namesake social worker and fight the typical battles and in a typical way that most would.

I wanted to be a trendsetter and show myself and the world a new example.

All the +Acumen courses helped me think about my life and how I could contribute to a better Me, better India and better World with my personal touch. God bless Jacqueline Novogratz, Marica Rizzo and others in the team. Learning indeed helped to overcome and deal with the tests of life better each time.

Expect great from God, Strive and Attempt great for God

Elders often tell me to pray a lot and have faith in God that the perfect things will come to me for study, work or marriage.

They expect things to come, without making right and calculative moves with good intentions to achieve them, forgetting that you have to "do Harkat to get Barkat." (Harkat means actions and Barkat means blessings and impact.)

This is what I had understood before my life changed at 23 (in case of a woman mostly):

"Be good by praying a lot and staying at home, obeying every word of the elders and following norms, without practicing what you preach. Miracles will happen and life will be good, family will be happy and you'll get the blessings of elders."

This is what society wanted and taught me. I again thought to myself: "Something is not right. This doesn't feel right. These older people talk but their actions say something different. I have studied my religion and they contradict that too as religion says to "tie your camel and then trust God.""

Society and elders were neither following the religion nor listening to their conscience.

They must be told through example what was more ethical. There were certain aspects of life where they might question or point out that the way adopted by me wasn't or isn't ethical but in the big picture and compared to their practices and actions, it certainly was and is. I told myself: "Society will know someday what is right as it is not wise enough yet to see the wisdom and the big picture."

When elders spoke ill of another community or group or about family fights, negative incidents or argue and shout or speak rudely or use very "polite foul language" I would say: "This is why the world outside is bad. You complain and wish for the Day of Judgement when you don't change your attitude and actions. Imagine such small battles we are fighting when people are dying outside. We must think and act big."

Doing the above often now, my folks are getting used to me and sometimes repeat my dialogues and even follow it!

I am trying to lead by example by not fighting every battle, there has been some change in the way my family thinks and behaves. I see my impact in the house too. That is leadership at home for me.

To expect great from God, you have to make great things happen and strive for and attempt great things for Him.

At 23, I was scared as I was told with the passing age, I would not get a good man. I was scared I would never find the man of my dreams and for my dreams. One day while ironing clothes, I heard the song "It's the Climb" and several others.

I thought to myself: "I'll take the plunge! What if I die while I'm young and single? What if the person I loved died or was separated from me? Do I have no purpose in life?"

I decided to surrender to God. I did not want to fight with the people I loved and those who loved me.

I love my family. I wanted to do big things and at that time it was to travel the world, to play all the air and water adventure sports that scared me due to a phobia of height or water. I wanted to climb a mountain too, a real one.

I wanted to change the world and create a legacy. I just knew education and women empowerment were my domains then and nothing else in details.

My intentions were clear as to why I wanted to do something big. First and foremost, I wanted my family to be ready and to be the family of dreams, for my brother to be a man of dreams for the woman he would respect and marry. If I didn't give up and my family saw me doing things differently from what majority or in fact every woman had been doing and is doing then there will be a shift in the mindset of my people. I wanted to do it for the woman I did not know but I knew she mattered. I wanted my family to be an example among families, that the world would look upto. Leadership at home was very important to me.

I had said no because I had the bigger picture in mind already. I said no for marriage to boys and families they liked but I knew were not good for my dreams and my dreams for humanity and my country. I had nothing to lose. I was already a Rebel but with a Purpose. If I fought my battles wisely for God and His People then I knew I'll witness miracles no matter how big the challenges or how tough and strong the opposition is. I knew I would win eventually and see the victory for humanity too. The battles I fought with myself was giving up all unproductive activities- partying, hanging out, fashion, movies, vacations, luxuries etc. that most youth would crave for and fight for. That made me more serious than I was.

I didn't bother to respond to jokes or understand them even if people laughed at it. I stopped spending a lot of time on dressing up and adopted a very simple lifestyle with fewer luxuries and desires that a typical youth or woman my age would have.

I spent wisely from my own hard earned money. I greatly reduced chats, gossips, backbiting and arguing with people unless it was related to my dreams and if it acted as a barrier towards fulfilling it.

That had decreased too but each time my focus got sharper and arguments and reasoning stronger as I was getting more and more serious about life. There were times when I told myself: "You are hurting your loved ones and disobeying them. They did so much for you and this is your return. They stood by you and you are opposing them."

But then again I told myself: "Madiha, your people are good and they will understand someday. Those who have negative tendencies, they will come around and your progress will change their attitude towards you and life. God will give them patience and heal their hearts. They will be proud of you someday in this world or the Hereafter. Today, you will have to be firm and impolite if required, for the purpose that God created you for." This worked. Things started changing gradually. Those barriers started reducing and I was able to start the journey of becoming the woman of my dreams.

The battles I fought personally I knew I could use these good deeds I did for God's sake when I was in trouble or danger or when I needed a miracle. Few of the good deeds that I have used already and which I feel would help others understand better is picking up the dead body of a puppy in a crowded place where cars were going over it and no one bothered. I told myself: "Madiha, some Muslims might point out you are doing wrong or sinning. I knew my faith better. This poor little baby deserved a proper covering and it's cruel to walk over or drive over it." I found a cardboard nearby. I took it and lifted the stuck and smashed body from the road with its intestines hanging and the smell of it making me feel like throwing up. It touched my fingers. People were watching me. I took it to a nearby gutter and covered it with other things nearby. I found a tap and washed my hands. I felt great because I did what felt right and so many elders saw it.

I had to be an example. I didn't care about what people thought anymore.

I had to listen to my conscience and do what's going to make me sleep peacefully at night and contribute to a Peaceful World. Another time at college, after my period and gap due to illness, when I returned and was covering up for studies, we students were all in the laboratory. One by one they raised an objection on different topics and incidents like my bringing Quran to read on the way or for issuing a certain library book and keeping it long which was a misunderstanding as well as my absence required me to cover up. One girl accused me of saying the "b" word to a certain community I didn't belong to and according to her, on the phone I said when I was angry at her because she was late during teachers day and I as event head and batch representative insisted that she comes early just like the rest to take out gifts from her locked cupboard. Another Muslim girl in the class said: "Madiha, I'm also a Muslim but they all respect me. I respect everyone." I felt so strange. I was wondering aloud: "Was this happening because I was popular in college or because I was leading sports practice in marching and starting cricket or because I organized a successful earth day event in college with my class?"

I knew where it was coming from. I told that girl from my batch who accused me of saying the "b" word: "If I die today then I'll die peacefully knowing I've not hurt anyone intentionally and this word I've never used in my life. Can you say the same about yourself?" She was quiet. I carried on: "In my school days, my seniors would say that how could someone not use foul language. She indicated it was uncool but it never bothered me. In fact using words like stupid, idiot, dumb was not part of my vocabulary except in rare cases for learning or reading. It is impossible that I could say such a word that you accuse me of. Go and tell the teachers and no one will believe you. Everyone knows me. You are telling a lie." Weeks later, this same girl was walking on the road near the college and it was raining. She stayed near my house. I told her to hop in and insisted out of concern. She agreed. I saw the guilt and our conversation was soft and gentle.

A group of people once hurt me and betrayed me. They had a problem when I distanced myself from them. I didn't reply back to their accusations because I felt it would be a waste. They didn't know my intentions or my thinking and every detail. So I told myself: "I'll focus on myself and be the change." Now when I've done that, I see curiosity from their end about my life and they say things like: "How did you go this far?" or "When is your talk being uploaded?" or "She will find a boy for herself." They seemed eager to get me married and maybe through their contacts. At one point in my life, I loved those elders but when I saw the reality, I knew it was a trap.

Sometimes when people that your family trusts get things arranged and fixed then they have control and influence, they want to spoil your life and I knew trouble would brew in that case. I was now able to identify people and distance myself from people who were not good for me or my growth and game. While I was associated with them and contacted certain people for work, I didn't get responses but now when I invested in myself, I see those very contacts messaging or liking or commenting on my work or impact. Strange world!

I didn't need anyone to make me successful. I needed God and myself and very few people and with them too very little dependency or not overdoing it to be successful or to start my journey and fulfill my dreams.

I told myself: "Madiha, there is no reason to fear or withhold yourself if you think and feel confident that the battle is worth fighting, that fighting it will bring glory and victory to humanity. Attempt great things and God will send you great miracles and make great things happen for you. Select your battles wisely. "

Battle of the 4 I's

In my own life, I faced and fought major battles of the 4 I's.

First I- Income

This has been one of the major battles in my life.

I wasn't getting a job of my type or the salary I deserved. I had conflict at home when I was exploring the idea of a job from 6:30 AM-12:30 PM, six days a week far from home which would take 30-45 mins one way and it was in an area we hadn't gone often in the past. I myself didn't want to work under a lot of restrictions, rules and kill my creativity. I wasn't willing to take financial help from loved ones even if they insisted.

I'm working hard and I have faith in God that I'll have more clarity and financial independence gradually. Financial independence is very important to me for my freedom, for me to contribute to society and economy of the country and for their progress. I have dreams of traveling and the first time I paid for my travels was the Spicejet ticket to and from Surat for the award ceremony. I had started my journey towards financial independence two years ago and I had traveled in Spicejet only, when my grandfather was undergoing cancer treatment. I was still confused but had taken the flight. I was writing in 2016 when I was in Surat for a week. I took a photograph with the crew in March 2016 and did so again in February 2018. It was a coincidence and one of the pilots said: "I flew her twice." She remembered me. The only difference this year was that the crew was all female. I also realized that Spicejet and I had certain things in common:

1) Popular among people

2) Looked upon as average

3) People from all backgrounds could afford and access its services

4) The 2018 trip gave me another reason to relate to it- women empowerment

5) The speed, the flight reaches before time and in my case, I'm known for talking, walking, thinking fast as well as being ahead of people my age or ahead of times.

I hope to travel more places in Spicejet for my book launch and to places of my dreams for adventure, to climb more mountains and conquer them, to make more dreams come true by inspiring and facilitating for others through my work.

Second I- Influence

Society will offer resistance to a person of influence.

I have faced challenges being an influencer inside and outside the home as well as while trying to influence people for impact. I have risen above the challenges that these people who make fun of me face and I don't fight battles that are not important in life and they are fighting but not getting results. My advice seems meaningless to them. I feel hurt when they do that but I know they will learn and they are human too. When I'm upset I tell them some things unknowingly but I'm also the first to apologize and very soon after the incident or conversation most of the time. My own elders especially the "modern" ones would tease me and say: "Why you don't know how many packets are at home? You stay out all day. You learn to cook, stay at home too." This is false as I strive to strike a balance.

I wonder sometimes why people think that my dad is conservative when he may sound or look like one (though I doubt it!) when he is more open-minded than the men in the family who say say that they are modern and support men and women or education and other things. Some elders say: "She is getting out of hand and I was like her in my youth but now I regret." This is false too as from his own narration of his life I gathered he was a rebel as a naughty boy who created trouble and fought a lot. He has regrets because of lack of purpose and following the "cool" trends and society or pleasing people. I am very different that way.

My purpose in life is clearer and I don't fight unnecessary battles. I realized that a person who is influential outside home, it will influence and change people inside too but I will also be on the receiving end of negative remarks and behavior as everyone looks back in the past and present and wants the same glory but not everyone is ready to fight and make sacrifices.

Being a person of influence, a lot of people contacted me for collaboration, events and parties, for meetings too. In one meeting, a person kept telling me: "You have the spark. Be an entrepreneur with us and you will be rich and independent." I didn't like the vibes, words or tone. I said I would consider but gave the signal of not being interested. After a certain event, a lady very fond of socializing insisted we hang out and party as she found me adorable but I said no as I would waste time, energy and get distracted. Another time, few influential males called for meeting for social work but I didn't get positive vibes and I didn't trust them enough based on how they behaved. I said no. I did not go.

I didn't and don't believe that as a woman I must work only with and for women as I am born to serve humanity but I would have to plan well because of the messed up state of gender interaction in the past and present in the world. To change it, I must understand as well as research well to bring in effective practices and techniques along with practicing what I preach. I am blessed to have mentors, mentees, friends, colleagues, collaborators who are males and whom I trust, who have won my respect and I have won theirs.

I believe my impact will not be complete if I leave out 50% of the population be it in terms of learning, working, collaborating or serving. We treat each other like human souls first and then the gender tag but yes being real and practical we take precautions and are aware of the challenges. At times when I feel doubtful or get a friend request or have questions about males, I talk to male friends and colleagues and they share, suggest or help me understand or deal with things. I believe in balance and I don't think a world dominated either by men or women will be progressive. Both need to be partners and collaborators, we need to support and back up each other.

I've never believed my role as a woman to be a weaker or easier one. I've invested in myself to take on tougher roles and share the table where the food is served and where the conversation happens. The meals and conversations are getting better and bigger so that as a woman I can influence lives not just through back-end jobs or front desk roles but on different levels of a pyramid and in a deeper and bigger way to reach greater heights and conquer greater mountains for myself and India, my nation and of course for humanity at large.

Third I- Immersion
One of the struggles that I've suffered a lot for is Immersion at different stages of life.

I believe in immersing myself in a situation so that I can give and receive more out of it. Even with people, I believe and I want to know their stories so that I understand them better and contribute to their growth, build trust and great relationships.

In the last few years, having worked with national and global projects and people, I've felt strongly due to my experiences that the majority of the Indian population isn't ready for "immersion" of this kind yet and that's why I have faced challenges. The curiosity to learn is often interpreted as wanting to steal ideas or contacts. I felt this for one organization I applied for work when I asked questions to be able to contribute more to the social problems at hand. Another time talking to boys and men for work in a religious organization, was considered as flirting and "wanting to talk to opposite gender" when they were themselves quite "free" with the opposite gender in spite of being "religious."

By being an example and continuing to immerse myself with people and places, I am setting a trend and striving to be the change. I'm already seeing the impact. My intentions are good and I believe in building meaningful relationships for impact, irrespective of gender, background, qualifications. I don't care about what society thinks of this anymore.

God matters more. What God thinks about me matters more.

I withdraw from people and places when I see no growth in me or them or the world around us as a result of that association or collaboration.

I'm also learning to immerse myself in a balanced way so that I don't get too attached and feel hurt later.

I think of the best and the worst cases and then act while immersing myself with good intentions and giving my best. That way in case things go wrong or out of hand then I have had God's protection or help.

In one orphanage where I had been volunteering for quite some time, my family complained that I was getting too immersed and I would end up being hurt or disrespected or my work there won't last long. I, however, kept immersing myself through activities to understand those I serve better.

Yes, I was told by ladies to "resume later" but I also witnessed great things later when a new president joined who respected me and whose leadership I admired. I had the trust of many respectable males and got nominated as sub-committee member while being connected to other members who were really keen on working hard.

Another example of immersion was when I worked for an organization for several years and due to personal reasons when things weren't good,

I resigned. I was hurt because I had literally given my life to it and then became on the receiving end of hurtful words and actions, accusations that shattered me.

Later I saw attempts being made by some colleagues to connect with me but I no longer felt it worthy. I learned a lot over those years but I also learned to not give my heart, soul and loyalty to a person or company so easily without testing them and always choosing the purpose and cause over person or company. Due to tests in life, in case things go wrong or out of control then I wouldn't be losing time getting over hurt or depression.

Fourth I- Innovation

I realized I was an innovator rather a social innovator because I ended up creating new ideas, beliefs, theories, solutions to social problems or at times gave a new perspective to an existing idea, concept or situation.

During my TEDx talk and preparation, I understood that better. This characteristic and talent of mine was a problem for many people. They said: "She comes up with her own things. Why can't she shut up? Why does she have to act over-smart?" Many people mocked me or made fun of me. Very few people were receptive initially.

I also realized that an idea is not enough. I have tons of them.

Since I immersed myself in every situation, people or places or activity, I have more innovative ideas but they need to be given enough thought and tested for practicality and sustainability. I am still learning to develop ideas and see which ones can really make an impact through action without discarding other ideas that do not make sense immediately or work out immediately. I write those down so that when required or at some point in time later in life, it could be used or developed or it will give insights to better ideas and turning them into actions.

REFLECT:

1. Look back at your life especially the last 1-2 years when you decided to stand up or speak up. What made you stand up and speak up? Why did you do it?

2. After reading this chapter on "Inspiration 5," how would you define battles, how would you define standing up and speaking up? What new insights have you developed?

VI

Giving up or giving in for someone or something

As a woman, I sometimes feel like sacrifice is inbuilt, as if it's ingrained in us and the spirit of sacrifice is preached and demonstrated since the early years.

Most women live their whole life with the wrong ideas of sacrifice and society is happy when a woman does not have clarity as she wouldn't stand up or speak up. She would make sacrifices, make compromises and adjustments or step back when asked to.

I had a problem with that at 23.

I wondered why a woman had to make sacrifices alone, why could a boy study and excel in his career before and after marriage, use his talents and education, skills and passion to serve humanity while the woman was expected to not do so and be there for the household chores alone?

According to me, both are equally responsible to serve family and humanity, fulfill their life's purpose and thereby bring about balance in the family and society. I also saw how most fathers were working and busy in business or service all day while the mother looked after children, their upbringing and fulfilled the duties towards the family. A man after being tired or at the end of the day or on a holiday, would sleep or rest or did as he liked but a woman didn't get that right or opportunity, time or freedom to do the same.

Most women would not ask or share their feelings, most men would not bother to ask or take turns as they were "earning for them" or "feeding them" or "looking after their needs and wants" or the family elders would also not speak up as "This was how it has always been." I saw too many cases like that.

I knew for sure it was not right, it was not just, it was not ethical. A child deserves the best of both the mother and the father to be a balanced individual.

Here are some of my reflections on sacrifices:

Culturally right may be Morally wrong, Culturally wrong may be Morally right

A lot of practices by society made me ponder on how "just, right, ethical and wise" they were and what may be culturally right could be morally wrong. Examples of practices by society that it justifies as ethical and wise could include:

-the system of dowry among the poor and the rich considered appropriate

-women studying or working being a problem

-marrying someone who was younger or much older or divorced or widowed considered as inappropriate or shameful

-being a single parent as a taboo

-being single or being a stay at home as a problem

-girls and women not allowed to have a voice or opinion or dictated and dominated by others as a practice or rule for generations

-strong and educated women being looked down upon as threat and family breaker

-bringing up boys and girls differently with respect to rights, freedom and opportunities

-women being restricted to house because "men cannot control or they get distracted" or it was unsafe

-being extravagant and spending beyond your means was a choice

-wasting blessings and resources

..and so on.

I also realized what may be culturally wrong may be morally right like:

-encouraging interaction with the opposite gender from an early age and learning to respect them

-having productive conversations and activities at home, school, college, university, workplace, community and party so that the sexual aspect is reduced relatively from thinking or conversations or actions

-giving voice with proper understanding and training to express in a dignified way to children, teens, youth, men and women

-lessons and training before wedding on relationships, economics, marital conflict awareness etc.

-lessons and training on parenting to equip the couple to learn child psychology, spouse relationship with children

-child rearing or skills training

-effective platforms to learn, share and exchange struggles and ideas to be productive at different stages of life.

I didn't want to spend my life making sacrifices for what was morally wrong but culturally right as I saw many elderly feeling regretful later on in life or when they feel in the hereafter. I learned about cases where people felt remorseful on their deathbed.

I wanted to understand sacrifice and make sacrifices so that I'll be successful and not sorry in life.

Making sacrifices to be successful and not sorry

Life is short and uncertain therefore every action must be analyzed as much as possible so that you can achieve more success and feel satisfied with your life, thus creating a legacy.

Talking to my grandfathers in the past, I saw regret in one's life and pride in the other's life. On analyzing their words and actions- past, present and how they spoke about the future, the decisions they took and their thought behind it, I learned that some sacrifices make us sorry while some make us successful.

I knew what kind of life I wanted. I was inspired by the grandfather who fought the right battles and stood his ground fearlessly in spite of setbacks. I've never seen regret in him because it felt like he lived a content life, doing his best while striving for what is right and just. I knew from his life about what kind of sacrifices I wanted to make.

Making sacrifices was a conscious act and it has to be a responsible one, well thought and considered. I've seen people make sacrifices to look great, for fame. I have also seen sacrifices being made for a cause, for a bigger picture in mind.

On social media, I enjoy reading posts and views on sacrifices by Alima Ashfaq from the UK, Naadira Chippa from South Africa, Dr.Tahseen Khan from Canada, Fatima Asmal from South Africa, Dr.Farida Khan from Mumbai, India- their stories inspire me. They have balanced views on life, women empowerment and success. They inspire women around them to fill their cup first before pouring other's cups at home or in society.

I believe in making sacrifices and I do make them for success, not for feeling sorry even if that means feeling sorry temporarily for being deprived of a luxury or privilege or fame in the short term. I have made sacrifices by saying no to some people, organizations and projects under the guidance of my close friends and mentors as that would make me feel sorry in the long term and not contribute to success in my life or for humanity in the big picture.

I will continue to do that as I'm a changemaker, born to serve and transform myself first and then people and systems.

Sacrifices- longing and lasting

Sacrifices are difficult to make either because you don't have the right concept about it or the decision to choose the longing and desire of the heart is greater than the decision to choose the things that last.

Most youth or people, in general, will give in to society's pressure to make sacrifices- for parents, for family, for society even if it causes more harm than good in the long term.

Many people say yes to a career they don't want because the pay is more, the family wants it. On one Facebook post, a boy messaged me for help. He narrated his life story and his dilemma to help him decide whether he should board the train in a few hours or not and do what his family wanted him to do and be. He kept telling that he was good at something else and he would earn well if he gave it a shot but his family insisted that he followed another "more noble" career as his family had many professionals from the same field.

He knew what to do and what to sacrifice but the next day I saw his post, his hidden pain in the words and sharing the joy for following his dreams, rather his family's.

Another incident is of a friend who was going to end up making a sacrifice to make his parents happy by marrying the girl they wanted. His reasoning was he didn't want to argue as his priority was work and profession. For marriage, he would let his parents choose as love and marriage was a distraction for him. His best friend stopped talking to him and ignoring him seeing his state. He postponed marriage. I asked him out of curiosity for my research why he was following so many youth and being like them when in professional space, he was striving to stand out and not go with the flow. He seemed to push the idea of marriage as he had lots to do that was more important then.

In the above two cases, the desire to please family especially parents was so great that both these boys were not thinking of the big picture and what would last and matter more. In the first case, if he chose to follow his heart and pursue what he was passionate about then he would be happier and earn more, he would grow more and contribute more to the world, get more popular and successful.

In the second case, if he chose what he wanted and what was good for him, what made him happy would in the long term make his parents happier, his impact in personal space would be more too and his vision and mission in life fulfilled.

When I reflected more on these two cases, I was left wondering about the extent to which girls must be suffering and their dilemma if "society didn't spare the boys."

I wondered how young men and women in spite of being taught by elders to do what lasts, were being forced by elders to follow the society's or elder's desires and they were going against their own children's happiness and growth. Even God's commands and disobeying Him in some cases just to please society.

Unfortunately, even "educated" and "religious" and "respected" people get trapped in this. It makes me sad to think that those who have influence can influence society but they rather fall trap into society's trap and things remain as they are. Blame game continues. Suffering continues.

The vicious cycle is repeated. Year after year. Generation after generations!

If only elders had more wisdom and courage to do what is right for God, to do what matters more and what lasts longer then how happier and more productive youth would be.

If only youth had more courage to take a stand for God, for humanity and for themselves and to make the right sacrifices and saying no to others including family or parents just to see them more happy in the long run.

By saying no to the longing and desire of their parents and not giving in to their pressure, by saying no to the easy pleasure or success or love, they could get what they truly loved and deserved, if only they thought more and gathered more courage and waited a bit more, God would send them miracles for choosing the battles wisely and making sacrifices for Him.

I pray sincerely for these elders and youth.

To make sacrifices for what your heart longs and desires or what your loved ones desire is easy but to make sacrifices for what lasts long and what's going to bring you and your family long-term pleasure, success and happiness is challenging, tough and totally worth it.

Not everyone can make these sacrifices though because the struggle is greater as is the success.

Greatness is not easy. Legendary is not easy.

Don't want to but have to

There are several things in life that I didn't want to do like exercise, taking care of health through proper diet and sleep or working hard daily but I had to as I wanted to be the woman of my dreams.

I loved chocolates, desserts and savouries. I loved staying up late at night. I loved food. I loved sleeping at odd times and rest. However, I loved something more and I wanted something more than I wanted the above things. I had to make a choice and decide what to sacrifice- these things or my health and therefore my dreams and that of becoming the woman of my dreams. I joined the yoga classes and gym initially but later went to the gym only. For several weeks I stopped going completely due to work. I couldn't exercise regularly at home owing to work. I would feel lazy and unproductive, sometimes sleepy too. I still ate chocolates if tempted to or felt weak especially Cadbury products- Flakes, Walnut Whip, Bubbles, Silk and others. Those chocolates made me stay up and work extra. I was getting worried about my health as I was putting on weight. I couldn't stop eating sweet things but I could replace or burn out.

I started traveling more by public transport, buses and autos as that required walking and sometimes I got down close to the venue but at a point that required 5-10 mins of walking or more. I had to take care of myself and nobody needed to know my sacrifices back at home initially in case they got concerned about my getting tired. I did not use my private car as my driver would complain and made me hurry everywhere. I was used to door to door service, the comfort and luxury all these years. I had to learn something I had not in the past but now I would learn. I learned to use public transport, mostly bus, auto and taxi in case later than 6 PM or on a Sunday or if I went to a new area far away. It helped reduce the harm and pollution to the environment. I got opportunities to sit, walk and stand with people, the majority in the country and see their struggles. Once while I was crossing the road and broke rules by using phone leading to a fine of INR 20. I henceforth tried to be careful on the road and tried to follow the traffic rules.

Seeing me two older men followed rules and waited for me to cross the road when the vehicles stopped. They were standing a little away from the zebra crossing but on seeing me they came next to me and then crossed the road.

Once on my way to the library, a man and a child entered the bus. There was no place to sit. I saw that the child was finding it difficult to balance and his father struggling to hold him. I told him with arms open: "Come. Sit on my lap." He did. I felt good as both trusted me. On my way back home, I was standing for some time and then got a seat. Soon two females entered, one older and one younger. To the younger woman, I offered to hold her purse on my lap and she gave me. I saw she kept tugging at her t-shirt in the bus to cover her hips as her back was facing the men's seat. I stood up and felt uncomfortable for her. I stood up and told her: "Now it's your turn to sit." She seemed surprised and hesitated. I insisted and she sat down. Another time when I was going to conduct a workshop far from home in the morning to a remote area, two mothers with their kids (both were less than 4 years of age) got in the same auto as me. They were talking in bengali so I asked the girl in bengali if she wanted to sit and took her on my lap. Her mother said, "I am surprised she sat on your lap. She never does in bus or auto. Kids identify people." That was a huge compliment from a stranger about my character that children are innocent and they can identify people as they are. The boy was standing so I took him on my lap. Both were the same age and size and they both sat calmly on my lap, to their mothers surprise! That made my day!

I've always seen people very engrossed in their own selves inside the bus or busy arguing and fighting upon trivial matters. I make it a point to create an impact and see its impact. I wanted to set an example and practice humility, the grounding that was needed as I climbed higher on the success ladder. I started seeing new things, feeling new things and doing new things.

I never had this experience or exposure before and I didn't want to stay ignorant. This was fun and better than the luxury of the car which I didn't want to learn again or drive yet. I felt happy walking as I got fitter and healthier and the chocolates, desserts were no longer harming me as such. My health issues were being treated easily. I started enjoying the weekly workout at the gym while listening to motivational songs. I didn't want any small talk, gossip or backbiting and that's why I went there as soon as it opened. I had earphones plugged to keep me focused and away from distraction. Regarding sleep, I started sleeping around 1-1.30 AM which was a bit earlier than my previous time of 3 AM.

I wanted to sleep early for good health and to keep dark circles away. I started feeling fresher when I slept at 1.30 AM and got up at 7 AM. I took power naps during the day if I felt tired. I was getting used to the work I was doing and things were getting clearer. Around late 2018, my sleep timing changed to 11-11.30 PM and waking up for prayers around 5.30 AM to start my day on a positive note, to ask God for courage and help to fight the right battles. I would sleep after prayer till 7 AM to help with housework before leaving for my workshops. At this time, my clarity was greater about leadership at home and work, about balancing life and relationships with the help of my best friend.

I stopped the frequent tea and coffee consumption after dinner or biscuits.

I was eating fruits or drinking natural fruit juices as much as possible. All these sacrifices helped as lifestyle changes led to positive changes in life. I learned that if you wanted to do something but otherwise didn't feel like it and that may be good for your health then you have to find ways to make it interesting and engaging for yourself so that you can do it and have fun too.

Being honourable and making sacrifices

Many times sacrifices may be made with ill feelings and with little clarity. It could also be made with lack of good intentions. An example could be a woman often reminding her husband and children of her sacrifice or people reminding their maids and staff of their favours on her. This is not being honourable or acting with dignity.

Along with the sacrifice, dignity is a must. The language used, the facial expression, the tone of voice, the behaviour before, during and after the sacrifice are very important.

Many people especially the youth think that using foul language is cool and therefore they often use the words in their daily conversation when they are angry or frustrated. I've never understood the need for foul language because I believe in being a dignified and peaceful person.

I've often noticed elders at home or on-road utter foul words in their mother tongue either for fun or friendly chat or when they are too comfortable with people or when trying to act rich, popular or when showing off.

When I hear youth uttering foul words in English then I feel that both are doing the same thing.

I realized I had to be more ethical and had greater responsibility. Thus, I started becoming more careful. I also objected when people I knew used foul language in front of me. I disliked reading or watching content that had foul language as I feared it would pollute my soul and system.

I couldn't allow that otherwise my impact will be reduced and God will also be displeased with me.

Making sacrifices for my dreams and to be the woman of my dreams required me to have dignity and carry myself in an honourable way. I was so happy to get an award called Woman of Dignity International Award in Surat and to share it with 49 other honourable ladies like Advocate Priti Joshi from High Court, Dr. Binny Sareen from Mt. Abu and others. I remember the words of Advocate Priti that being modern didn't mean you would forget our Indian values and principles. I believed the same.

I believe that a way a person dresses, walks, speaks, behaves, even thinks, must have dignity. This helps to increase the depth, height and width of your impact. Of course, you will make mistakes and I did but I started my journey towards reformation and transformation immediately.

It's not about not making mistakes because that is impossible. It's about making them, accepting them, admitting them and reforming yourself as soon as possible and rectifying the mistakes. It means to work hard to be better each day and have a better day and be better than the day before.

As human beings, we may have high moments and low moments as a result of which a person's actions and thoughts, words and behaviour may vary a lot. I believe it's important to keep striving and being present in the moment, being conscious, knowing your limits, doing what's best for you and humanity and staying true to yourself and God.

Sacrifices- Easy to die but difficult to live

A lot of people wish for death, to die for something or someone they love, thinking it's a big sacrifice they would make. Dying for someone or something or a cause is noble and difficult but what's more difficult is to live for it.

Living for something or someone you love or a cause is much more difficult as there is more effort and pain at times but so is the pleasure of success and satisfaction. A lot of youth I talk to and learn about, they tell me they want to die in peace as it's easier compared to arguing with elders, family or society about their dreams and desires, even if they being young are right and more ethical, their intentions and actions more noble. This struggle in girls is more for their dreams, going out to study, work or marriage and for boys, it's mostly about the choice of career or spouse. In either the case of boy or girl, it is possible that the struggle may be due to a family conflict they have been witnessing since childhood and they have wanted to express their feelings and sufferings and are unable to.

I too have had moments when I thought death was easy. I would think of asking and praying to God to end my life. I soon started to realize each time: "That's like acting average, a loser, an escapist. I am none of that. If I live then I can use my talents and gifts, work hard and create moments of satisfaction and success, create history and legacy, make the world and myself exclaim: "Wow!""

I never shared this with anyone except my best friend as I knew elders would judge so again I had to teach myself and analyze myself what's right for me and humanity. Even in my college days, I loved interacting with other girls- juniors, seniors and peers, to know their stories, give them hope and see them brighten up, their eyes shining and body language that reflected excitement. The confessions pages which have no proper or productive use often disturbed me. I came across one, after an incident that happened during marching practice of my department and stream. I was leading the practice as an assistant to a senior for the first year and next two years as lead and therefore I would have rightfully been the flag bearer on the final day.

The day I along with some peers was deciding the final squad and mentioned my leading the squad, a girl with a badge, in the council who wasn't regular at all for practice objected and said she would lead. She was forcing it. I knew based on her behaviour and nature, there would be a big fight. I didn't say anything. My friends from other departments, Saheli, in particular, insisted that I should speak up as I deserved it and should have it.

I refused to fight even with tears in my eyes. She informed her head of department and one professor whom she trusted more. I had won their respect. I had the love and respect of my squad. I didn't want to fight as I had the cricket tournament to lead that year. That would be the first year of the official cricket tournament in college. I had my third-year exams.

A fight would disturb my peace of mind and productivity. We didn't get a position in marching but I didn't see that as my failure. I knew for most girls, marching was a one-time thing and therefore my focus was needed on what mattered more. That girl with a badge respects me today. I had come across the confession pages through my newsfeed and posts from my friends.

I knew God proves who the better leaders are over time.

Curious to know what affects my age group, I checked a few posts and quickly closed it as I didn't want to read and know too much. I understood that there were posts on breakups, heartbreak, gossip, character assassination stories, suicides and hardly anything positive.

Living is difficult and living with honour and dignity even more so but totally worth it.

Sacrifices and Pleasures of Youth

Youth is a time when I'm often told to enjoy more, be less serious and act my age. I have often struggled acting my age as per society's norms and concepts. It's not that I don't feel like it or don't have the desire but I feel guilty and irresponsible doing so. I saw my batchmates having boyfriends and with whom they had a physical relationship with and with whom they could do all that the soppy serials and dramas showed. I saw people my age hanging out and spending hours in undignified activities with the opposite gender, consuming drugs and alcohol, smoking cigarette or hookah, having illegal sex, gossiping and backbiting, having the "time of their life."

Parents often have concerns about children regarding these and in spite of great attempts, they fail to protect their children or put restrictions on them. They fail to protect because children carry out in secrecy then fall into trouble. They end up in situations that shatter them and their children.

In many cases, I've seen children and youth falling prey to unproductive and undignified activities due to parent's irresponsible behaviour like over restrictions, lack of understanding and empathy, quick to judge attitude, lack of respect of their "what will people say?"

Students from good and popular schools and educational organizations indulge in these undignified acts more than those from low income or underprivileged ones although it could happen everywhere. This along with my own experiences showed that the well to do families where children have everything at their disposal, no shortage of things they need, suffer a lot and that too silently. This is why I do a lot of workshops with this crowd.

It is my belief that if the hearts and minds of these youth are at ease and peace then the wealth in the pocket and resources of the mind and body, internal and external, will be better used for serving the country and humanity.

I feel sad to see "educated, popular and influential" people encouraging smoking that is harmful to the body, soul and environment. I don't see the sense and logic behind considering it cool. How can someone be so careless and foolish so as to cause their destruction, disease or death?

I see people especially youth wanting to look and be "modern and educated" by consuming alcohol. I know of many stories of how alcohol destroyed individuals and families and yet people don't learn or change the behaviour. When I met a few people from the west, my friends who were Christian by faith telling me they don't consume alcohol and their reason behind it, I was happy to know them.

They told me they didn't want any intoxicants in their system, any unhealthy substances inside them. I remember reading a tweet by a lady I admire a lot, an IPS officer against alcohol. That made me happy.

It's becoming more and more common to promote and advertise it, very popular figures are doing it. What's worse is that heroism is associated with alcohol.

It's great to see youth and elders who are firm about their stance on things, beliefs and actions especially against something that is not beneficial, that the majority indulges in but which is harmful in the big picture.

Regarding the opposite gender, I really believe there must be a physical distance rule in place no matter how modern the society becomes. If there are no rules then there will be corruption in society and biological or psychological factors or both could lead to unproductivity and harmful outcomes for individuals and humanity. I don't think and believe that interaction with the opposite gender is a problem as it is natural and inevitable. The problem lies in the fact that the youth are not trained at home or school in dealing with the opposite gender. They are too shy or too over expressive and therefore there is a communication barrier and wrong messages get conveyed either way.

Another problem is that youth are often unable to talk to parents about the opposite gender as openly as they would like due to the generation gap as well as lack of understanding on both sides or either side.

Communication between the opposite gender is taken negatively and unnecessary. Those that have productive conversations also play the hide and seek games to protect themselves from unnecessary attack and moral policing.

I have learned something due to my interactions with males as well as other females that there are some youth around me who are more ethical than the elders and the rest of the society. Conversations with them is soul food and helps me grow personally and professionally.

I'm blessed to be surrounded by such youth who have a focus in life, interactions with them and the mindfulness and consciousness during our conversations is something I've seen missing in most elders and fellow youth. That makes me ponder on how wrong society is about youth. These youth are leading by example and being a role model for fellow youth as well as elders. Being in the company of such youth, I too think and act differently. It's wonderful how we can talk about anything, on any topic with respect, dignity and maturity with each other, irrespective of gender. There is a kind of concern and protective nature towards each other and towards the nobility of our souls to serve humanity in a better way. We do our best to hold ourselves accountable, help remind each other and advice each other to keep the conversation productive, friendly and focused on building meaningful relationships as we are a family of changemakers who are trying to be role models, to be the winds of change and if we fall into the same trap and turn into problem creators then who will solve the problems and offer solutions, who will be the solution? Our views on every part of our life is different and unique from the typical one that society and elders talk about or misinterpret and promote.

It's not that we are perfect or we don't desire the pleasures of youth. We keep reminding ourselves and each other of the bigger picture, what matters more and of the nobility and impact of our work and thereby reducing the desire to indulge in unethical, unproductive and undignified activities so that we continue to be impactful in our cause, on the receiving end of God's help and miracles.

REFLECT:

1. What kind of sacrifices have you made in life? What kind of sacrifices have you seen people around you make?

2. What are your thoughts on Sacrifices and Intentions, after reading this chapter on "Inspiration 6" and how are you going to make sacrifices or intentions henceforth?

VII
Yes! Why? No! Why?

Whenever you take a fun quiz online or see notifications on your device, yes and no is sometimes an easy task, rarely do we give it a lot of thought.

However, in real life, yes and no is crucial as it can make you feel proud or humiliated, happy or regretful, complaining or grateful for a long time or even eternity.

Here are my thoughts on yes and no as a young woman who said yes:

What society wanted

At 23 and even earlier, I realized society wanted me to make a choice and if I did then I heard: "You are always hasty and impulsive and then you regret. You are too young to decide. You don't want to listen to elders. We have seen the world more than you have. It's not as easy as in the books and lectures."

Society wanted and still wants me to say yes to being average, to be like the rest, do what's safe and "right," "obey elders in everything," follow the typical path that the majority traversed and that was kind of known, stay in the comfort zone, to lead a "perfect life," to end up happy while destroying my soul and humanity."

Any talk of study and work was feared as the man is there to provide while a woman to follow orders and do everything she is told and their way. At the end of the day and her life, she is to offer pleasure, very rarely herself feeling the same as women and men are not given proper sex education at any point. Society says no to that.

Society wants a woman to say yes, to being average by encouraging her for learning, practicing and earning through the common skills of cooking, sewing, baking, selling beauty products, clothes, footwear, accessories, crafts and arts for all and do as much as possible and only from home.

Teaching and in fact tuitions at home was the "best" option and profession. If a woman thought beyond this then she is asked: "Why do you have to do all that? Can't you do from home? You'll get tired. It's unnecessary. Do you have a shortage of anything in life? It's not like you have to support a family. Why can't you get more tuitions at home or teach?"

When it came to applying for masters, I was told: "Why not do B.Ed as it will help you teach?" I said: "I could get that in future, why would I do another bachelor's when I can do masters and go to the next level and upgrade myself?"

Society wants a woman to say yes to "do what's right" according to culture and elders, like sitting in big groups and talking about how ignorant or miserable or inferior another community, culture or religion is and that too in religious gatherings and places sometimes. They talk of how the neighbours or relatives are acting foolish and have no sense at all, that they do no good and are sinful.

They talk of how careless youth are and that they don't listen to elders, to not go anywhere during the month of fast or do anything much besides kitchen work and prayer, what latest things to shop for and where, the problems caused by and evils in maids, staff, in-laws, uncles, aunts, their families, kids or relatives.

And what's shocking to me is while talking about them and about such things, they add words of prayer like "May God forgive us and guide us all!" or the "world is such a bad place, people so sinful and misguided and shameless!"

Society wants a woman to say yes to obeying elders and elderly who may threaten and emotionally blackmail about dying if their cultural wishes are not fulfilled. They would give loud reminders in their own voice or others videos on obeying elders and being respectful at all times, showing gratitude and forgiving their shortcomings. It wants her to say yes to their desires and promises made to others for marriage or power games and matters of cultural pride, to say yes to every concern they have and the advice they give. They want her to follow their orders, to always ask and do everything they want. I have seen young men going through this too.

Society wants a woman to say yes to the typical path traversed by the majority and ridicule every soul who doesn't and then claim superiority over them. I've heard them say: "She has done her studies till bachelors and works from home now. Good. If she studies too much and does too much then where will you find such a boy matching her personality? In our community, it's not common and why think of another community? If only today's boys and girls understood and married their own cousins or from their family or relatives. We obeyed our own elders. Today these youth, they say: "We are brothers and sisters. We want our type.""

I have also heard: "Is she learning cooking and cleaning? And housework?" or "It's her age now to marry. Get her married. By now, she should have kids and be well settled. As she will grow older, it will be difficult."

Society wants a woman to say yes to things that are "safe," to not go out or stay out after 6 PM as it's not good, to say yes to going to places of study or work only nearby and not too far away as they were unsafe due to distance or unfamiliarity. It could also be that the driver would leave the job, the elders would suffer and panic.

Society wants her to say yes to meeting people who they know well, who they approved of, who they considered safe, to go to places, study, work and pleasure that they approved of, irrespective of what is good in the long term.

Society wants a woman to say yes to lead a comfortable life where the man provides or she could work from home only and look after family and kids first and then anything else. It wants her to say yes to a perfect life where she compromises, even accepts and adjusts with physical, verbal or mental torture as the society would say: "The girl couldn't adjust, her parents didn't teach her, she is not matured or wise."

Society wants her to say yes to win hearts of elders but at the same time advice her that a mother-in-law and daughter-in-law will be that way. They will treat her the same as it has always been and she should do the same.

Society advises her to obey her husband but at the same advice her to control him, to keep him under her or he will lose interest in her. It wants her to control her thoughts, words and actions, dictate and then say: "She cares for them which is why she is behaving this way."

What society did not want but I wanted

Society didn't want certain things that I realized I wanted and that each of us in this world deserves and want.

Society wants a woman to say no to improvements as it takes them out of their comfort zone, results in the status quo being questioned, challenged and disruption leading to change which is very uncomfortable at the beginning at least.

When I took bold steps to say no to not giving in to the traditional norms or any corrupt practices, I was told: "You don't have to be over smart. Do it." I would simply say: "Okay. Thank you. I'm over smart. I don't feel it's right. I won't do it." I didn't stop others from doing it but I wouldn't do. Why should anyone then have a problem with that?

When I refrained from corruption and politics at home or outside then I was told: "She is diplomatic." Sometimes people bring up the past and say that I did what I wanted like sleeping or eating habits or demands as a child or caused trouble. I would reply: "Past is different. Nobody told me then about the right and wrong. I had no role or say in things then. I had no role models to show me the real big picture. Today, the world is also different and the problems are more complex, people smarter. Children have more confidence, boldness and knowledge. You can't handle it the same way."

I actually study and learn about the behaviour of people-adults and kids, about leadership and parenting, relationships with spouse and parents (both parents- current and future, not calling them in-laws) so that I can understand and do better when I take up these roles.

I wanted to be better and serve as a role model to the society by learning and practicing the improved techniques backed by research.

Of course, I would err but how I would deal with failures and mistakes will also serve as an example to them.

Society wants a woman to say no to uniqueness, to greatness and "wowness."

At 23, I realized I wanted to be more than average as average was boring according to me. I wanted to find the uniqueness in me, find things that I was good at and great at, things I sucked at, to improve them or learn from others and work with them to complement my skills and talents and to complement theirs.

Society feared that and I was sometimes told: "Don't share such big things and big names as people (read as a potential spouse or in-laws) may not like it." I was surprised at how much society wanted me to downplay, to not fulfill my potential as it was threatening to the others. I didn't do to show off but shared and felt pride in the investment I made in myself. It feared a woman who was strong, intelligent, powerful, unafraid, had a critical and analytical mind of her own, who had the courage to speak up and stand up for what she believed in.

Society considered her a threat as an empowered woman who would break families and destroy its peace. I thought to myself: "Society really does not want an empowered woman." I'm grateful to God and TEDxBESC team led by Mr. Dilip Shah for the opportunity and belief in my story. I shared my views as an empowered woman, to remove common misconceptions that society had about her that made them hostile towards her and made her suffer verbally, mentally and physically too.

Guilt and Regret

A woman who does not say yes and says no to what society wants then she is made to feel guilty and regretful.

Many times it succeeds to do so. If it doesn't then it makes every attempt directly or through people close to the woman and in her immediate circles.

Society fears a truly empowered woman and therefore it can go to great extents to control her, check her freedom, clip her wings because her victory could according to them lead to downfall of their corrupt cultural practices, to the evil they benefitted from by showing it as just, good, religious and for their well being.

They fail to think such a woman will reform and have a better and happier life and even something God will be happy with and that humanity will benefit from. At one point, I also felt guilty and still do when seeing my loved ones suffer or concerned or worrying, unhappy and stressed but then I think of the big picture for myself, humanity and them.

Looking back, I realised that I felt guilty and regretted at some point saying no to certain people or things but upon reflection, I became more peaceful and realized that the choices made then, resulted in the life I am living today that makes me happy and impactful, makes those same people who judged, criticised, objected, these are the ones whose behaviour towards me has changed.

Today, I see more respect in their eyes, the tone of voice and words, desire to meet me or do something with me or maybe go out or work together or dine together.

I then feel: "How can I trust and let this society make me feel guilty when it gets carried away, blown by every wind that blows their way and has fickle minds that change very quickly?"

Decisions and Choices you make

You may often consciously or unconsciously let others make decisions and choices for yourself. You may not intervene or object because that is again comfortable and convenient for you even. You would not have to see or go through pain, suffering, hardships and struggles if you do as you are told, go with the flow and let others "older and wiser" make choices on your behalf.

I was okay with that when it came to food, furniture, utensils and accepted advice on devices and clothes but for study and work, my dreams and future decisions that really mattered, I heard the society and elders but took time to process, weigh things then did what I felt and knew was the best for me and humanity, after consulting God and my mentors.

I was amazed at times on how society and elders can make you feel loved and cared for through right words and actions but when you reflect and connect things, you'll see the game and agenda. It's not that there is evil in that all the time but the love and concern, protectiveness, fear, anxiety is so much that it dominates their systems totally and you may be influenced by that a lot of times.

I remember the words of an adult who told me: "You will never get and have everything perfect."

When I did not feel satisfied while making certain food items thereafter I thought to myself that this same adult often talks of perfection in food, clothes and household matters. How is it then that this very adult fails to see and think of perfection when it comes to more important things in life like study, work, cause, relationships, impact and legacy?

I knew that very moment whether I should pay heed to the words or not. I was deeply disturbed that day, very gloomy and sad. I heard motivational videos and soon felt that if I acted that way then I was feeling guilty as society expected and I was behaving the typical way society does and I have to be better and more ethical than them otherwise how can I serve them and lead them better.

I believe it's important to make decisions and choices for yourself but it's not easy and not everyone can do it. I could not do so until last year even if I said yes to my dreams in early 2016.

Over the last two years, I have acquired many skills through my interactions, study and work with people globally, self-study and reflection that helps me make better decisions and choices than I did before.

I learned to make mindful choices rather than based on feelings alone. My heart tells me something, my brain tells me something and my conscience something. I learned to use all three to analyze if it will be good for me, humanity and my family in the long run or not.

I also try to imagine the situation in action and try to understand how it feels. If it gives me a sense of satisfaction and peace or brings a smile to my face and a sense of pride then I go for it. I make a small prayer to God almost immediately to guide me and help me. I renew my intentions and recall my "why" either silently or loudly by looking at the sky or in prostration or anywhere. That gives me a lot of courage and confidence.

I learned more about the things or ask people of experience and expertise to share their views and opinions, for their critical feedback to help me make informed decisions. I often do so from various and diverse sources so that I could compare and analyze better. While taking decisions, if people make me feel guilty then I often think about death.

One day, I saw an ambulance passing by and it struck me that if death was near then would I do a certain thing or not even if society was against it? I told myself: "If I die while I'm young and single then all of their concerns are meaningless. It's just the marriage and the spouse and his family's thoughts that is making them act this way."

I also believe when your intentions are good, your actions are aligned with it (every effort made to do so) and you gather up the little courage you have and if you feel guilty or have doubts and even then you keep striving to do the right thing and moving forward, it is then that you see signs and miracles from God.

The day the elders told me about doing the right thing and that I needed someone to guide me, I saw signs that day. I met a beggar, an old lady who came to me and I said: "Forgive me." She went away with peace and an understanding look. I saw her go to two other vehicle drivers. I called her and gave her more than I ever gave another beggar on the streets as I was impressed. She explained with such calmness and dignity: "When people tell me no, I quietly go away."

I visited a college for inquiry about masters courses and usually found old, grumpy people working there. A lady came out of the office who very politely answered all my queries. The place, the office, the system etc. made me feel happy. The same day I visited after coming across a Booktique which had a publishing house too.

I knew these were all signs from God to stay unique, to not give up due to the pressure from society even if they were making me feel guilty by showing lots of concerns.

I knew I was doing it right. Signs like these affirmed my beliefs and gave me confidence.

Purpose and Meaning in Life

The fairy tales I grew up reading or listening, the movies and books that are enjoyed by many or become best sellers often highlight the quest for love rather than purpose in life. That is what society does too.

From the teen years, it focuses on equipping and framing or molding the woman's mind to be on the quest for love and then punishes, scolds, ridicules the youth when they do so at a time society does not want and when and with whom it disapproves of.

Society wants a woman to say yes to love more than it wants her to say yes to purpose as the "right and perfect" match and catch would mean a perfect and successful life. To achieve and attract the perfect catch, society might droop low and very low sometimes, sacrifice dignity and respect, indulge in unethical and corrupt practices too.

Society however chooses to ignore the importance of purpose and meaning in a woman's life as somehow the message I felt it gave out was: "Your purpose in life is to be the "perfect, obedient" daughter, sister, granddaughter, daughter-in-law, wife, mother and follow the traditional path laid down for you, the ways of the elders and do as you are told by them, even if that is against the Lord's commands. You must excel in household chores, child rearing and relationships "the way" we tell you."

It says that but the advice and suggestions that are given after that are quite contradictory and as a result, there is a great deal of heartbreak and suffering in the family and nation!

Being an obedient and perfect woman through the different roles imply to give in to dictatorship, blind faith and following, to give in to harmful practices for the sake of pleasing loved ones, to not care about the souls and humanity's progress and growth and only do "what seems right."

Excelling in child-rearing and relationships implied controlling people, to make them follow certain rules and act on things that may not be just, ethical or leading to peace. It's more about doing, having and being what they want rather than arriving at a win-win situation or build meaningful relationships with good intentions.

Having a purpose and meaning in life will give you the courage to stand up to anything. It will help you make informed and conscious choices, to get clarity and critically think with an open mind and for the greater good for yourself and humanity.

I realized my purpose in life over the last two years slowly and steadily and it happened through learning and doing good quality personal and professional development courses from +Acumen mostly, reading articles, watching videos especially TEDx talks and some pure motivational talks, by interacting with people from diverse cultures and mostly virtual from across the world through Lifebushido, OpenIDEO, +Acumen, social media accounts.

I spoke to all these people via chat or email or call, learned about their life stories, how their life changed and looking at the patterns I started making my own observations that are helping today with my own life, work and cause, to give better examples and insights on life.

Most people had several twists and turn either in personal or professional life or both and the journey had lots of struggles, confusion and mistakes. Amidst all that, these people chose to not give up, to not be like the rest, to not follow the typical path. They were not happy or focused completely but they started the journey.

Different questions helped me at different times. The speakers who inspired me were Dr. A. P. J Abdul Kalam, Mel Robins, Tony Robins, Oprah Winfrey, Rick Warren, Nick Vujicic, Muniba Mazari, Malala Yousafzai, Sandeep Maheshwari, Robin Sharma and others.

The +Acumen courses on NovoEd and Udemy had exercises and activities that made me think and reflect on my life. I am blessed to be a part of this community and to have access to such resources. My mentors played a big role too. Dr. Tahseen Khan who helped me overcome my fears and advised me to create short videos as did Advocate Priti Joshi, Nazir uncle for sharing his ideas and suggestions on social entrepreneurship, Pulkit Vasudha and Stuart Price for the advice on not settling for little and to have a focus in life. I learned through their example of parenting and true love too.

Steve Kantor gave me great practical tips on the importance of paid work, balance and goals in life, Dr. Anil Pradhan on time management and prioritizing then putting time, energy and resources accordingly.

Late Yusuf Dinath, my maternal grandfather gave me this advice: "There is nothing to fear. No one to fear but God. Fear God and do what's right. People will then fear you and know that you won't tolerate or give in to the wrong things." Jawwad Patel gave me great motivation and insights on powerful intentions, having focus and big goals and dreams, never settling for little, to think beyond normal. Iqbal uncle helped me deal with my internal fears and doubts, by sharing his views as a parent.

A friend from UN on the importance of servant leadership, simplicity and knowledge and suggestion for courses, a friend from Pune on optimism and being practical.

When fear or anxiety would stop me, I would think about what would happen if that thing was dealt with. For example, if money and resources are a concern then think about this: "Would you do what you had in mind and go ahead with your plans, if money was not an issue (either you earned it or had it or someone else gave it)?"

Another example is: "Would you do it if your family and society supported you and did not say the same things or behaved better?" or "Would you do it if you had the support of your spouse and in-laws?"

If the answer to the above is yes and you feel positive and hopeful then you must know that what you want to do "needs" to be done. Those fears and anxiety will disappear and mean nothing when you would have accomplished your goal, those concerns and critical components will stop mattering to you or bothering you or they will stop saying it.

I realized the importance of asking good questions when I joined Lifebushido, through my +Acumen courses where I learned and did coaching, through my life coaching experiences with people. For a women leadership summit, I was told that I would be a speaker and I was happy but even happier when not selected as one as I challenged myself to prove to myself that I could be a really good listener, ask good questions and not always talk but really listen.

Speakers like Falguni, Pallavi, Mita and others appreciated me and encouraged me. Many people who heard me in the audience messaged me, wanted to connect with me like the granddaughter of an ex-governor of West Bengal and a young man working at The Indian Chamber of Commerce.

I realized I'm getting better at giving feedback and asking good questions, critical thinking and analysis as I wanted to improve myself for the better and help others do the same.

What I said yes to

By saying no to the people and organizations at 23, I said yes to me, yes to my dreams and yes to becoming the woman of my dreams.

Over the last two years, I have understood the importance of saying yes to taking calculated risks in life, to being a global citizen, to being a lifelong learner, to being a multipotentialite, to not give in to the pressure from loved ones or society and settle for little, to be the best version of me, an "extreme" me as Sarah Robb O'Hagan talks about in her book to stay true to myself and God, to connect ideas and people for a Peaceful World.

Saying yes to things that matter isn't going to be easy at all but if you push forcefully the fears even for a few minutes by positive self-talk, keeping in mind your strengths and weaknesses, your passion then you'll win the battle eventually. Fear will stop paralyzing you the same way, your anxiety or in case of OCD will stop acting dominantly and to the same extent.

To me, controlling my mind is more important and I said yes to learning to do it and to practice it. By doing that I'm more successful in dealing with me, with people, contributing to a better world and making a positive difference. Of course, I fail and make mistakes too but I learn from them and not let my ego stop me from improving and doing better the next time, to learn lessons each time.

Controlling your soul is equally important. Society will tell you to abandon, quit, refrain, boycott instead of teaching you to deal with it productively and effectively. An example is in the interaction with the opposite gender. An all-male or all-female world is impossible. Instead of criticising the interaction between the sexes, I believe children, youth and adults must be taught how to interact with the opposite gender with respect, they must learn to collaborate and have productive interactions, on how to reduce, avoid and replace unproductive activities and interaction between them so that there is a conscious effort from all sides and less corruption.

What I said no to

Over the last two years, as I have grown up and I feel I did grow up more than I learned and did in all these years because of a life of luxury and protectiveness and where it was more of listening to others than my inner voice or to the powerful positive outer voices.

I said no to other people and organizations who were not good for my soul, who would reduce my productivity and make me less focused and serious about life and legacy, who directly or indirectly instill in me negative vibes and destroy my peace of mind and soul.

If I could not totally distance myself then I reduced my interactions with them, reduced sharing and activities with them, reduced happy or good moments that would make them talk a lot and express themselves. In case they did that, initially, I didn't sense it negatively and responded as a word battle and fun but soon showed disinterest and refused firmly but politely. It may seem impolite, rude, selfish and uncaring but my peace of mind was more important and I couldn't suffer huge losses of time, efforts and focus by trying to overcome the negativity that followed.

To me, preserving me and my soul, its sanity and integrity to the best of my ability were more important, only then would I be able to serve humanity and express my concern and love for the people, the society that was in need of it in the long run.

When I attended events or posted on social media, people messaged or commented, expressing their appreciation mostly, very few with negative responses. When it came to dealing with men, it was difficult to sometimes understand the intentions but thanks to my tribe of friends especially male friends whose feedback and suggestions helped.

Even while shaking hands, I had my own rules, not to shake hands each time with men who I met often. With men any time, I avoided physical contact as much as possible for personal and professional relationships. I didn't like men standing too close or hugging or holding hands or putting their arms on shoulders, waist or arms. I believed it was unnecessary and brought with it an unnecessary conflict that could be avoided.

I sometimes see a lot of youth doing and thinking that it is part of being "modern" but I feel it has nothing to do with being modern or open-mindedness. In the name of friendship, female empowerment and modernity, I sometimes feel a lot of unnecessary, unproductive and unethical actions are carried out.

Just because the younger generation often indulges in them does not mean it's not part of "society" and corruption as it's often assumed by the youth themselves that they are fighting the older generation and the corruption they cause.

A man commented on a quote and another time on my photograph and I immediately replied saying what was the point of writing that. He apologized in the comments as well as the inbox. Another time, when men commented on my photographs, anything personal like my looks then I deleted them. This led to reduced comments and gave out signals to people regarding my views and behaviour.

I didn't want the comments to distract me at this stage when I was laying the foundation of my legacy. Once a solid foundation is laid down then distractions of this kind will not bother me or I will be equipped to deal with it better. In personal space, I have more time for things that matter now and the goals to be accomplished.

I told myself: "Madiha, when you have achieved these goals and fought these battles in the next few years or months or weeks then you can do and focus on all this too that you wanted to do- makeup, clothes, footwear, accessories etc. Right now is not a good time. You can't fight all the battles at the same time and have answers to everything, to convince others and win at everything."

They required critical thinking and making choices. I was writing a book, starting a social enterprise, setting the foundation for some projects.

In the public space, my introduction at SCET in Surat surprised me. Two girls spoke of my inner beauty and my no-makeup look. This was a TED event and a prestigious college where students belonged to well-off families and had priorities and standards where priority was given to superficial things. Meeting some social workers and hearing through others or dear friends, I was very happy to know their views on me, my work and impact, their confidence and faith in me, their observation of my credibility and quality.

I recorded videos that were quite popular but they were too simple and of poor quality in terms of presentation but that showed how much people focused on content. I loved natural and simple things as it saved time, effort and money. This was a need and priority due to the choices I made.

By saying no to things that mattered less, I said yes to things that mattered more.

Since my intentions were good, I knew God was helping me and my impact was reaching more people.

I got a call from Aligarh where a boy said: "Ma'am, after watching your TEDx talk, it seemed like an average person was talking. We could relate to everything. We felt that if you can do it so can we."

It's not that I was against fashion or makeup but that I had a lot of choices to make and decisions to take and a lot of time would be gone thinking about matching clothes and accessories or makeup. I had just started earning so I had to choose where to spend money.

Minimalism helped. I was fighting many important battles and makeup and fashion could bring in unnecessary complications of beauty, boys, etc.

I had just started knowing the real world so I just wanted to focus on the most important things first. I told myself this time I would buy the bracelets and rings, shoes and bags, clothes and makeup, watches and earrings from my hard earned money.

Time and money are precious resources when you start a new journey and I being a Multipotentialite had a lot of things going on simultaneously so I needed a bit more than an average person who was say focused on one thing and their requirements.

I ended up saying no to less sleep that resulted in dark circles and health complications. Then my best friend explained in depth and in a way I could understand. I started sleeping early and my health improved.

I was taking calculated risks in life and when I made a mistake, I had a soul tribe of mentors, best friend and friends to guide and help me. They helped me through critical feedback, suggestions and ideas. This I believe is one of the greatest blessings in my life and a reward from God for saying yes to things that mattered and saying no to things that mattered less. I found my tribe and so will you if you figure out the yes and no in your life.

REFLECT:

1. What are the things in your life that you have said yes to and that you have said no to? Why did you say yes or no in these situations or cases? How did you feel after saying it? Satisfied or regretful and why?

2. After reading this chapter on "Inspiration 7," what insights have you developed about saying yes and no to the different things in life? Is there any particular line or concept from here that has stuck you and that you feel you can relate to? Why did you choose that line or concept?

VIII

You want it this way. Why?

All my life I enjoyed and looked forward to 15th August because it was either a holiday or school was over earlier than other days or there was a patriotic feeling listening to talks, singing songs and watching performances. The history lessons were fun too and Indian freedom movement was a topic I enjoyed reading about and learning.

I hardly paid much attention to be able to empathize with the people who fought for freedom while I was a student.

I knew it was not easy as a theory but never did I expect or imagine myself giving it so much thought until two years back and even now. The concept of freedom became clearer when I went through the personal struggles and still do.

Need for Freedom

The realization for the need for freedom came when I felt overwhelmed by external pressure from society to live a certain way and be a certain way and that I soon realized did not involve being true to God or myself.

It pricked my conscience.

I had a problem with that. This required me to compromise a great deal in every way, to be who I'm not whether it was taking photographs while exploring proposal to appear nice and perfect or live according to their unjust terms and conditions while disobeying God, forgetting my own purpose in life.

The kind of talk I heard from other families and my own, broke my heart. I had no interaction to understand the other side better or to explain my views. In a few cases, later on, I was the only one seeking clarity, sharing my story and views. I didn't like the typical way proposals or marriage was explored by the society. It all seemed so fake and superficial.

My fears and uncertainties increased and I didn't like most proposals-men and families. I observed all of them wanted a woman with a checklist and the items listed were too fickle or priorities were not right. That checklist was not aligned with my values and principles. It reflected their lack of focus and purpose. I knew I didn't want that and they didn't deserve me. I was not willing to settle for little.

If I agreed to every compromise, I knew I would regret it all my life, I wouldn't be able to face God or the next generation for being a loser and escapist. I always wanted to be a Hero, a Winner and a Leader, not an average.

Every year in school, I would imagine my name being called out for something big and my going up on stage to get the certificate or award. It never happened though. I knew I had to work very hard and looking back I feel it was easy then. When it came to life, I found it worthy to work hard and no matter what was required (of course ethical), I would do and be the hero of my life, create more heroes even if society turned me into a villain for sometime. It was not until class 12 when the election for student council was going on that my name was called out or for the Good Conduct Award or the Woman of Dignity International Award later on or the Shepreneur award in 2018, that my dreams of getting an appreciation for being the heroine of my life was coming true.

I wanted to stand up, speak up and fight for truth and justice, come what may but I knew freedom was important and I'll take it, if not granted or permitted. I wanted freedom in my teens to use the phone at night, to wear certain clothes, to go out with friends or on trips. I didn't fight hard then because I was not passionate about those things. I lost most of those battles.

At 23, the pressure from society resulted in an equal and opposite force rising from within me to fight for my freedom, against the injustices that were leading to no good to individuals or humanity in the long run. It's important that you realize and identify the need for freedom and then fight it as it will give you courage due to clarity and bring God's help due to good and powerful intentions. It will help you persist and accomplish your goals, to not give up in spite of challenges and conflicts externally or internally.

Why fight for personal freedom?

What I studied in history lessons about why people fought for freedom in the past was that freedom was the birthright, there was the feeling of loyalty and patriotism towards a state, country or belief or at times the need for power or control, sometimes negative and sometimes positive.

In my case, I fought for freedom like some others did in the past who I admired and who created a legacy.

I wanted to fight against and overcome the evil practices that controlled the minds and souls of the majority of the people. That condition was affecting me and that was the first time that I stood up for myself.

By standing up for myself, I knew I was standing up for humanity. I stood up, spoke up and said yes to start my battle, my struggle against injustice that was making hundreds and thousands of girls and boys, men and women suffer and often silently.

When the realization of the magnitude of the fight sunk in, I was gripped with fear and uncertainty. I had no idea what path I would take, how I would find the resources, who will help and who will oppose, who will be true friends and who will be fake and a threat.

All I knew was that this struggle and freedom was very important and it was not only important for me but humanity too.

I started believing in my good intentions and that hard work will bring God's help and miracles, how and when I had no idea.

I didn't know much but I knew it had to be done. I had to be the one doing it.

I realized: "To God, I belonged and to Him was my return."

The control that the family wanted made me think of the umbilical cord being cut during birth and that I was no longer bound to the body. As for the nourishment given to me while inside or outside the body, I would not be able to repay or return the favours but I knew I wanted to nourish their souls even if that required pain for them or me for sometime when they saw my behaviour and actions.

I would keep nourishing it through my good deeds, by being a legacy creator, by being a means of on-going charity after they leave the world so that they keep getting the reward and benefits. That was a better way I felt.

The death of several family members made me think about how the person we love is cut off from people around. I was reminded of a saying of Prophet Muhammad (peace be upon him) that when a person leaves the world, people and wealth leave him. It is the good deeds alone that go with him to the grave.

I was also reminded of the verses of the Quran that I studied in my teens and youth that parents, siblings and loved ones will be of no help on the Day of Judgement. I read that every person will get returns and rewards based on their actions, that actions were judged based on intentions.

I knew that I would be the solo rider and it was in the end and also all along about God and me.

I told myself: "Madiha, nothing will matter then. You remember reading in another verse that even loved ones will refuse to share their good deeds if you fall short of them to go to paradise. How can you let them affect you so much today and in this world that they make you forget your life's purpose and prevent you from living a life true to yourself and God? Today they are showing care, wanting to help, guide and just in case they are telling you cultural things or things that will cause more harm than good and if you don't process, analyze but accept everything then you are headed for eternal guilt and regret. There will be no going back then. It would be a matter of eternal happiness or eternal sorrow. If you oppose and fight for freedom, the right kind today, you are doing good to all. Even if most people do not change, you played your part. And God is watching. Miracles will happen. Your impact will grow bigger and deeper. Don't give up."

Ownership and Freedom of Loved ones

This is a serious concern in most relationships wherein you may want to control your loved ones as if you own them, as if they are created to obey you and follow you. I've heard folks say: "I worry so much as a (relation) and I can't stop thinking about what it will do to you. You are not being wise. You can do such and such things this way too. If I don't tell you then who will?"

I have seen husbands telling wives to obey orders, think, act and be as he wants. It is called oppression in simple and straightforward terms. I have seen husbands telling wives to go to certain places, do certain things a certain way. There are wives who dictate to husbands what to wear, what to do or say, how to behave etc. That turns into jokes or justified as a woman or man acting responsibly. There is a great imbalance in both types of cases.

According to me, if both give each other the freedom and space, if their foundation is on the right criteria and basis, with proper clarity and understanding of the relationship, the sooner the better and of each other then the outcome will be much better. Most boys and girls want to spend the time to "physically" know each other when they could instead spend time on more important things and save themselves from a lot of guilt and heartbreak.

I have seen parents telling children to make certain choices rather than giving them tools or helping them analyze and make better choices together. Most parents and elders in the family act like they own the children since birth and their control grows stronger and reactions super strong towards anything that weakens their control. They often want to know and have control of the places, people, days and timing, even content that the children associate with even in their youth.

This control is mainly due to the continuation of the age-old traditions, of confining to norms, out of the fear of what society will say and how people will perceive them as a result. Too often they end up believing others rather their own child even if they otherwise say there is trust and belief. This is because according to many of them, today's youth just want to rebel, they are not focused and often acting carelessly.

This observation may be due to the children not reading and performing theoretical acts of worship as often and in the way, they would do, forgetting that the sincerity and dedication is expressed and accepted through intentions and actions and the two being aligned rather than the utterance of words only. The words give you energy and reminders and have rewards associated with reading but they must be accompanied by intentions, actions and reflections for true success.

The confusion between Free Will and Fate

While studying philosophy, religion, talking to people, reading quotes and even books, I realized that I was confused between free will and fate.

Has God decided everything and I must go with the flow and wait for things to happen?

Do I become who I want to be and God has no part whatsoever? Do I let destiny unfold my life's purpose or do I take full control and do everything as I want, what I want and how I want?

While thinking about the answers to such questions the following words came as inspiration due to reflection: "It's more important for me to be socially responsible than to be socially acceptable if I want to be more ethical than the society and if I want to lead them to better ways of living or if I want to serve humanity better and be an asset to it."

Being socially responsible was at the core of my values and life principles, my work and impact so I realized the need to figure out and have answers to my confusion between Free Will and Fate.

I realized I had to "tie the camel first and then trust God." I knew that just waiting for things to happen wouldn't work as I would have no say or influence over things or what happened to me.

Blaming others seemed like being a loser to me.

All my life as a student, I saw that it did no good so simply waiting for things to happen would lead to no positive lessons or outcomes. I thought about doing what I wanted and how I wanted, with belief and faith only and the result was that I didn't get so many things. Nothing happened.

I realized the answer, the solution was to do my best, give my 100 percent with good intentions and renewing them whenever I could to keep me focused and at the same time to keep striving while praying to God to take care of what I could not foresee or control.

I knew the struggle for freedom was a big one and a tough one.

The social sector in my opinion and based on my observations and experiences seemed to bother adults and elderly due to safety reasons mainly. I started feeling that while I was working hard with good intentions and focus, I had some people around me who were not thinking, saying or doing all of these with alignment. They thought something but said or did something quite contradictory.

I thought to myself: "Many of them might be against me and who knows maybe planning against me. I am not so wise and there is no one so wise and great who can foresee, have knowledge of the big picture and look at my past, present and future, look and know how the world is. Not even my loved ones or society. I realized only God could do this."

So I would tell God: "God, I am doing my best. You know my intentions too. What I can't control, You please take care. It's all very difficult and even very painful sometimes. Please help me."

He would respond and I got answers and solutions, I got help in ways I didn't expect. I saw miracles and here I am today writing my story and this book. I understood that there needs to be a balance between the two extremes of complete freedom and complete free will. Following or believing either one will lead to failure.

I started realizing through my life observations and experiences and through others lives that God is All-Knowing, He created the world and us, so He Knows everything that had happened, that is happening, that will happen. He has given human beings free will, unlike many human beings who will not allow that and try to control fellow human beings.

When we make certain choices, we get certain outcomes.

He plays a role to facilitate or catalyze the process or to make it reach great heights and depths when he sees exceptional and great sincerity, hard work, nobility, persistence and faith. In my life, I have also seen Him not letting certain things happen as later I realized if He facilitated then I would be in a great mess and unhappy as a result.

Freedom and Boundaries- our own and others

While interacting with fellow youth during college as well as through my talks and workshops, I realized that there was often this dilemma about freedom of an individual and the dangers of crossing over into another person's freedom and boundary.

I thought about simple examples that I could relate to, like those of adults-parents or teachers wanting to exercise their freedom and insisting on what they did to be repeated or when they said they knew what was best for the child and therefore not asking the child directly or indirectly for small and big decisions that were related to them and concerned them.

When children are very young and innocent, they may need a lot of help and occasionally decisions may need to be made by letting them know rather than having a discussion on it. By 16 years or even earlier, I feel adults must start giving teens a lot of exposure and be there for them so that in the later years, they can make better decisions and informed choices about their life, about things that matter to them and the people they lead.

I realized that elders often wanted those younger than them to not "make the same mistakes" they did or others did, to not suffer too much, to not hear the negative from the family or society.

I thought: "How sad! They forget it's human to err, to make mistakes. It's real and practical that society will talk negatively even if you are the most careful, focused or ethical person. These things are natural and can't be avoided."

Mistakes can either be reduced by learning "what went wrong?" and practicing "how can I make it better?" and then the action on "I will make it better!" or learn from others mistakes so that you can make your own new ones and learn faster, do more and be more.

Children and youth must be given tools and mentoring but they must be allowed to make their own mistakes, to learn from them, explore and be their unique self. This is the reason why I started life coaching, public speaking and storytelling especially with the teens and youth, to mentor a few youths at a personal level and through my projects and work with more of them so that they learn by seeing me in action, learn with me and I learn and develop new insights as a result of those interactions. I give them certain tasks and then give feedback followed by suggestions to improve and take things forward to the next level.

People often overstep into others boundaries of freedom out of extreme concern sometimes that society would attack, criticise, gossip, backbite and they would have to "hear it all."

I learned from my own experiences in the past several years and in the last two years, in particular, that society will attack, criticise, gossip, backbite when you are wrong and when you are right, when you strive for the good and for the evil.

I told myself: "That is how society has always been!"

They like to complain, blame, attack, tear down character and reputation, do moral policing because that's easier and requires less courage, effort and brains which is why there are mostly average people and not great.

They do not want and do not like to see anyone doing better, working harder, having more courage, they do not like people who are putting more effort and brains for the good and doing right things because those people will become great and maybe popular than they are.

Knowing the nature of their fellows as well as their own, all of them will want attention and time of these great few and that might hurt the ego of the majority, it makes them feel guilty. All this is unacceptable, disrespectful, immoral according to them as it makes "them" appear as bad people, on the side of evil when all "they wanted was good for all." In the name of righteousness and nobility, overstepping into others boundaries, forcing their choices and opinions was allowed and justified.

In my interactions, I realized that I was at times stepping into others boundaries out of love and concern. I started by telling myself: "Madiha, you can't be like the rest. You have to be different. You have to be more ethical as the standards were dropping low."

I wanted to continue the legacy of the great men in my family, of the great men and women in the city, country and the world. I was becoming more conscious of my conversations in-person and virtual, ensuring I didn't overstep, that I gave people tools and suggestions but allowing them to go through their own journey and make their own mistakes, intervening when it got to extremes or heading close to it but very politely stepping back when I saw the other person was determined to do their own thing.

I wasn't angry with them or they were not angry with me at least not for long. There was mutual understanding and trust.

I remembered to write or say often: "Shout out if you need anything. I'm here for you. You can rely on me. I will do my best if you need any inputs from my side."

This led to a lot of good as I was improving myself, building great and deep relationships where there was understanding, trust and a win-win situation, in-person or virtual, local, national or global.

I learned from the mistakes I made in the past and used these experiences and lessons to make them my strength after more research and observation. The very long messages and emails started getting shorter, words which were misinterpreted or misunderstood were replaced by more polite or professional or simpler terms.

In case of conflict, a call was preferred over a message to avoid fights. Even then I messed up occasionally because I started seeing a new world and meeting a diverse group of people since only two years ago, in a big way. I was learning and evolving.

I was able to connect with souls globally and have conversations that mattered. I could plan actions that would lead to win-win situations often.

I realized that I had started connecting ideas and people for a Peaceful World. I saw that people across the globe could connect with me and my story. In the last 2 years, I started networking and meeting more people through very credible sources in the beginning so that I could learn better techniques in virtual global communication and where there was an accountability factor.

Over time, I learned to identify people I wanted to study, work or create impact with. I learned who to trust and whom not to, how to test and check credibility and character, how to keep testing over time.

I sometimes made mistakes but through "doing" I was learning faster, improving faster. My best friend was there for me when I was confused. After a productive discussion, I would get clarity incase I was stuck in some cases.

I learned to respect people who were different from me in many ways, from different backgrounds, culture, gender, culture, age, gender, geography, profession and priorities. I learned to co-exist peacefully, respect their beliefs and choices even if they contradicted mine.

It stopped bothering me too much as I got more clarity on improving myself, on who I wanted to be and who I didn't want to be.

Freedom of Speech

At school, I studied about freedom of different kinds and the one I often think about is freedom of speech. Society exercises this right fully and completely but won't let a woman exercise her right and freedom of speech. There was a time I used to like religious gatherings but then I stopped attending because they preached often about all the extreme ideas which are more of culture than religion.

The messages given out are often without context and background or without any references to cases where the practice or message differed a bit and an alternative path was taken. A very common example is when it comes to parents or women related topics.

I often saw the person delivering the talks sharing the reward for obedience to parents or elders but the majority will never speak about the meaning of obedience in details, in the context of obedience to God before any human. That makes the elders exchange looks among themselves and with the juniors. Sometimes I have also seen people who deliver lectures is hired by someone so that he or she says things to please that person or people attending it or that will bring a few or more "benefits in this world only."

In the last 5-6 years, I started looking at religion and spirituality quite differently but the practice became better over the last 1.5 years. I included what God really wants- reflection and application, not culture and theory as the society or the "knowledgeable" people talk about.

As much as I love words, I do not just speak. I ensure my thoughts and actions reflect what I say. I believe in being an example. I had to do and be. At least keep striving. It is then that I witnessed miracles.

Sometimes I feel that the reason why I studied pure science is to understand religion and science. That the observation and inferences are important. Thesis and research are important but without the "thinking beyond normal" and "powerful intentions" and "faith" to keep doing in spite of failures, there will be no miracles and breakthrough innovations like my best friend has witnessed success.

With professional success, there will be personal success. With increased profits, there will be an increased impact. I learned this through my best friend's example even better.

Studying science with faith gave me an eye and vision for details, to plan out and do what most people dreamt but thought as impossible. I addressed a crowd of eminent scientists and scholars and masters students in the

University of Calcutta in a National Conference when I wasn't a masters student even but a Bachelors in Botany.

One of the professors from my college invited me to speak on corporate social responsibility and I delivered a talk titled "Re-Search the Soul." She got to know about me through the feedback of other professors and principal on my talk as a Chief Guest on NSS Day Celebration where I shared my story.

After seeing my posts and photographs, a junior from school contacted me to organize a talk on social work in one of the top institutes for social work, IISWBM in Kolkata. I realized that in terms of degrees I was not qualified to talk or "preach" the crowd that was more qualified than me, be it the national conference or the social work institute or even parenting campaign by Junior Horlicks.

What made me stand out was observation and empathy followed by research, reflection, application, innovation along with upgrading my skills and knowledge.

Being a multipotentialite makes my talks more effective and successful in the work I do across different domains. I was blessed and I am blessed to get very positive feedback from the educated and the ignorant, the rich and the poor, the traditional and the modern, the kids, teens, youth, adults, elderly, the intellectual and nerds crowd as well as the fun-loving crowd.

Many people would make fun of me or laugh at me for being talkative and talking unnecessarily at one point of time but I turned that into my strength so that people would start knowing me for it. My talkative nature landed me in trouble a few times but mostly good has happened as a result of it.

I realized people speak a lot- on social media, on TV, rallies, religious gatherings and even at home but most did not use this freedom wisely and productively. It was bringing a lot of harm than good in most places which is why I wanted to be the winds of change.

Speaking up and standing up for truth, justice and peace for all brought me respect, popularity, appreciation and support from around the world and it also brought taunts, criticism, hurt and pain from far and near.

However, I believe because of my intentions with hard work and my being the change, changed a lot of people who were otherwise considered as narrow-minded or conservative or those with no hope. I was happy and grateful to God that He gave me these opportunities to change lives through speech and for guiding me to use it wisely and productively and giving me the courage to apologize or reform myself when doing it wrong.

There were times when I was rude or impolite, insensitive or harsh but I was usually the first to apologize if I was wrong and also if the relationship was very important to me. If I spoke up for something right or against wrong, I didn't apologize.

Internally though I would tell myself: "Madiha, you can try to be a little more polite. You can lower down your anger and frustration and be a bit calmer the next time."

When I would feel bad, I would talk to God: "God, you know what I am doing and why I am doing it. If I give up and let my loved ones or people older to me decide and do what they want from me or for me then not only I but humanity will lose. None of these people are evil but just culturally driven over the years, pressurized by relatives, peers, society. God, please guide them and console them. Please give me the courage to keep striving and to not give up or give in. I am weak and feel overwhelmed. With You, I can't lose. Without You, I can't win. Please help me, guide me and make miracles happen for me so that they and the world believes more and sees the truth, justice and peace win, so that humanity wins."

God did respond in His Time and in His Way, sometimes quickly and sometimes delayed but I learned that He does respond if you call out to Him sincerely with a humble heart that shows desperation for His Aid and Guidance.

Freedom and Leadership

At the orphanage, where I had been volunteering for over 3 years, after my personal transformation, I wanted to change my approach of volunteering from random activities to concrete activities with transparency, records and reporting. I started counseling, created a format based on experience and piloted the model.

After taking weekly sessions over 6 months, I trained 4 more females to conduct these while I was supervising. During these sessions, I identified certain needs and challenges which I proposed could be fixed through a House System in the residential setup where 6 challenges would be the duties.

I took permission from the highest authorities and started forming a team of high school girls for primary school kids and college girls for secondary school kids. This was due to several reasons- I wanted more girls to learn from me and with me. I wanted to create more leaders and wanted the girls at the orphanage to be surrounded by role models who excelled in academics, extracurricular activities and who were well mannered. I wanted to be more accountable for my work and cause, wanting my impact to grow big and deep.

Also, I feared that if I did all this alone, I would become very powerful and sometimes misuse the power, use phone or be unproductive sometimes as no one was there along with me. But if I had many people under me, who I was responsible and accountable for and to, I would fear God and people and more could be accomplished.

I started building trust as a result of my work ethics and professionalism especially among male members. Few female members showed objection, made efforts and ultimately stopped the activities I conducted. I got tags of being power hungry and others. My folks then said: "We told you to not get too attached or over-do. You don't listen." I said: "I didn't do for anyone. I did what was right. That's it." A few months later, I was called back with great respect and in April, I was nominated as a Sub-Committee Member.

This I believe was a result of my ideas and practices of leadership which was observed and appreciated by genuine leaders and uncles I respect like Jameel Uncle and others. Jameel Uncle is a great leader because of his leadership style and how he supports others who want to work and do. He knows the importance of freedom, accountability and teamwork. I admire the leadership of Steve Kantor who likes to have control of the big picture and small details but believes in delegation of tasks, accountability and building a global community of interdependent people focusing on their life goals and unique talents.

I do believe in teamwork and in mentoring juniors to lead, to create more leaders and delegate tasks but I also believe in the leadership style which I share with and admire and respect in my best friend, where you as a leader are trusted more as a youth, so many a times it is a one-person army. It is because you are multi-talented, excelling in many skills and efficient.

After a down phase in one team we were a part of, one of my friends and I had a great discussion on the need for one leader who has the big picture, clarity of vision and mission, who drives others and prevents the cause from crumbling down or from corruption or from going off track or from being influenced by negative forces.

I like to have things clear and in one place after taking inputs from others, letting others do their part. The reason I believe in the power of one is that I have seen causes and initiatives crumble and crash after a high start where few wanted to take on top leadership thereafter. I do believe that there should be one person on top who has the final say in matters of the organization or cause and this leader develops a system of transparency where he/she feels accountable to those who he/she leads.

However, in relationships, especially in marriage both man and woman must be partners and neither must dominate the other. There could be times when one leads the other but both must go through times of leading and following so that there is a balance and the relationship grows stronger.

Virtual Leadership and Freedom

Lifebushido is greatly responsible for helping me develop my leadership style in virtual communication and during virtual collaboration. I started to build good relationships with changemakers virtually, locally or nationally and globally. In a virtual setup, there is more freedom, more chances of misuse, deceit and danger but over the last three years doing it each day has taught me a lot.

I have learned to identify the good people that belong to my soul tribe, a family of changemakers, friends and collaborators. I found my mentors and mentees too. I have learned to have a grip on what the conversation is about, how it goes when something doesn't feel right, I either shared it with the other person and we had an open conversation and we resolved it or I simply reduced or stopped responding to messages, stopped liking or following certain people.

Virtual communication has taught me very different things about leadership and leading myself and others. Most of my work has been virtual so far and most of the people I work with, they are either remotely situated or our communication in the same city is virtual.

In the years to come, I will share more on virtual communication and leadership.

Awards and Recognition

A lot of awards these days have self-nomination option or they have the option to nominate others.

Some people object to self-nomination and some nominate the undeserving. Some people raised questions about the credibility of a person receiving the award. All this made me think of how freedom is misused, resources wasted.

Self-nomination is fine if you know you deserve it and have worked for it. Many times people say: "It's better to work sincerely without awards." It is like saying that if you get an award then you are not sincere or you are showing off.

I believe as my scientist friend, said in one of his videos: "Don't make the award the focus." This was after he got the National Award by the Government of India. He says: "Find a problem. Give it everything- great intentions and hard work. Award will come as a result."

Recognition, praise, popularity, influence are outcomes that are not bad or destructive if the intention is good and the foundation is solid.

As humans, we all desire approval, appreciation and recognition. You must do all you can to keep yourself grounded so that you are not carried away by them or start using them negatively or unproductively.

These awards and recognition must be used to improve the work you do, help you take things to the next level when you have more confidence, more resources, more networks to tap into, more people to reach out to and more lives to change.

Why I want things a certain way?

Once during my workshop in a school, the management after confirming the date and time refused to do it for the students. They gave several reasons rather excuses and then said, "Tell your boss or whoever that this cannot be done."

I was startled. I said, "God is my Boss. I came here to do the workshop for the students, future leaders of my country. It will help them. I scheduled it for today and did not do other things as this was important. I will do it and go. Tell me where I can do it." After almost an hour of discussion, they agreed.

During setting up, they complained that there were not enough chairs or space for all the students in the class. I picked up the tables and chairs myself along with my team and arranged it in a way that the full strength of the class could fit in an average size room. Then there was the problem of time and space to do activities. I modified it and still made it fun. The teachers and students had a great time! The administrator who earlier refused to allow it, later asked me (full of smiles): "I heard it was good. Our children liked it." He was taking feedback from a teacher. Teachers were happy too.

On other occasions during my work for different projects, I always spoke up and shared my honest thoughts and ideas out of concern. This courage and confidence comes with my belief that I have no boss but God. He is my Boss. I report to Him directly and therefore my actions or words or thoughts reflect that.

Even for relationships, I keep reminding myself that I am not in control, that people do not belong to me, that He is the One everyone reports to. There is no scope for fear, jealousy, insecurity, concern. He is in control and everyone reports to Him.

REFLECT:

1. What kind of a freedom have you desired in the past? Have you achieved it? What kind of freedom do you desire as of now? Why this freedom? How will it affect your life and the life of people around you- country people and humanity in general?

2. Ponder on the different kinds of freedom people yearn for as children, teens, youth, adults, elderly. After reading this chapter on "Inspiration 8," can you think of a solution for each stage or as many stages of life as possible?

IX

Dilemma of More or Less

I have often been in a dilemma of more or less in different phases and aspects of my life.

Some people, articles or talks address this topic-some speak about doing more and some speak about doing less, some speak about laser beam focus and some on giving a chance to yourself to explore and excel at multiple things.

Some speak of living simple and minimal life and some about working hard and then spending on yourself as you deserve and worked for the comfort.

Minimalism

I came across the concept of minimalism via a TEDx talk by the founder of Becoming Minimalist in 2016 when I was going through a tough phase in my life. What appealed and still appeals to me about minimalism is that it gives me time for what I want more and what matters more. For example, owning less stuff meant less cleaning time and have more time for my learning or work or with people who matter and help me grow.

Simple clothes meant less time and energy spent on making choices for clothes and matching it and more time and energy for making important life and daily decisions. Makeup free look meant less time spent on external looks at a time when I was unsure about my purpose in life and why and how I was unique. It gave me more time to be my real and raw self amidst people and find ways to be more beautiful in different ways.

I remember glances in the weddings where I looked simple but I made it a point to stand out through what I loved- greeting people of all ages, giving them full attention and respect, having meaningful conversations, doing what most don't- building relationships even there and creating impact.

I decided I would keep aside a set of clothes for daily wear, a set for professional events, another set for parties and weddings. Washing daily and ironing each week or each time before dressing depending on my schedule then. In 2018, ironing is daily or every two days when my purpose is clearer and my schedule more balanced.

For some time I stopped buying clothes. For footwear, I had some 6-7 pairs and styles that I would match as they were comfortable and smart, that I could easily wear in a hurry or that gave me no trouble in public transport. For my hijab, I had kept some simple ones with neutral colours that would keep me comfortable in the heat or in cold. I wasn't willing to experiment too much even if people said I looked older than my age due to the style.

In the winters of 2017-18, I used to sleep on the sofa in my sitting room or on the carpet there and not on my bed so that I would have less time to change the sheets and cover or do the bed in the morning. Sleeping like that gave me the opportunity to see the sky at night and talk to God alone after a hectic day but a productive one. Sleeping like that made me sleep peacefully but not too comfortable that I forget important things in life especially with the air conditioner on. I didn't like it when in a room with my sisters, I had cramps or felt very cold or had to get up to switch on the fan or wake up from sleep to switch off a.c. I considered that a waste of time as I was already sleeping less.

I stopped making choices for food and demanding for food and ate everything that was healthy or easy to eat, made at home. Very rarely outside food. When I felt weak, I ate chocolates and then burn those calories through walking and using public transport. For transport, I stopped traveling in my car and instead used the bus or auto and walked more to keep myself healthy. This helped me overcome many of my health issues. My time, money and energy were being saved in dealing with illnesses and I was learning more about the majority of my countrymen and countrywomen.

I kept my nails small as I didn't want germs to fill in my nails or enter my system. I stopped wearing too much jewelry as I felt hot or hurt myself while working or hurrying or focusing while doing so many things as a multipotentialite. I also feared to lose the jewelry as I did when I was a child and teen.

For my interactions, I hanged out only virtually and with very few people on a regular basis to save time and ward off distractions of meeting in physical space. All the people I spoke to regularly, were friends like my family of changemakers and professional connects. Talking to them about work, cause and life helped all of us to understand each other better, to work more efficiently and create bigger and deeper impact together. I started spending my money wisely, saving it for things that mattered and that helped me grow.

I was spending my time wisely, doing what will contribute to a better me, better world, with no time for small talks, arguments, corruption or unnecessary heartaches.

I was spending my energy wisely, doing a lot of different things that made me happy and that made others happy.

I felt like dressing up and doing makeup and matching attires with footwear and accessories then as I did in my teen years but it was not possible. In late 2018, I can do it and I enjoy it too! I feel it is best to take things lightly and train yourself. It is important to prioritise things in life so that you can go further in lesser time.

You don't need choice in everything

As human beings, we make hundreds of choices- small and big, every day, intentionally or unintentionally. We are surrounded by our loved ones who love and care for us, who want to make choices for us. With too many choices around and too many choices to make, it can be quite difficult and overwhelming.

Not grabbing an opportunity and not making informed choices can lead to a lot of guilt.

What I have learned from my journey in life so far is that I don't need to make a lot of choices.

The best way to ensure that you make important and right choices well is to let go off the power to make certain choices that can be made by others.

In my case, I felt for food or furniture, I let my parents handle and make choices. I give my views on them but don't pay too much attention to them. I will focus on them though in the years to come as I want innovation in all aspects of my life and as I take on more roles and in different stages of life with different people in collaboration so that together we can be role models for others.

For clothes, my mom has a great taste so I take her along for shopping so that her expertise can help me make quick and better choices- colour, style, material, comfort. Before I select or wear clothes, I ask myself: "Will it look elegant and graceful? Will it make me comfortable and worry less about it and focus more on being present and on being who I am, helping me create more impact?"

For gadgets, I ask myself: "Will it serve my urgent needs of email, camera, notes, calls, messages, calendar, calculator, Whatsapp, opening docs, editing website, accessing moodle and courses?" I then looked at the cost and how strong and sturdy it was.

For me, the most important decisions in life were about study and work, dreams and causes that I cared for, at a personal or professional level, that I knew I could do justice to, excel at, contribute effectively to. Anything related to these was important and I ensured I had a full say and control of them, not letting anyone else choose or make decisions for me or on my behalf. Anything that affected these, I would stay away from so that my focus is not lost, my vision not disturbed, my mission work not slowed down.

It was not at all easy as my biological systems sometimes desired to act natural and take over but I knew I had to have control over them or they would control me. So if I felt like watching something that was not productive like a movie, drama or song, I would force myself to listen to motivational songs or talks that would energize me to focus and think big. Having said that, rarely have I given in but most of the time I have succeeded in refraining and each time I have refrained, my will power the next time has increased and improved and temptation reduced.

This results in the mind not giving so much thought to it or taking it too long to make a choice. Alternatives may pop up in the mind or the thought can easily be pushed aside. Staying away from listening or watching unproductive stuff helps to keep interaction productive with the opposite gender too.

Less is more

In some cases, less is more. When I was writing for my speech for TEDx and I sent my bio to a friend from OpenIDEO in the UK, Kate, she said less is more.

Looking at a friend's portfolio, an international personality I suggested to make it minimalist for some cases and we both agreed on keeping it bulky for some other cases.

My own style in the last few years has been in accordance with "less is more" where I started wearing different colours and clothes that looked simple but I got feedback that they were quite elegant and graceful. I also realized by the way I carried them and without or little makeup. A lady messaged after she saw my photographs: "How do you pull off a makeup-free look so easily and elegantly? Come and have a meal with my family."

During the award ceremony in Surat, I did not have the time to dress up due to my tight schedule and work so I went directly after finishing 3-4 meetings and a quick lunch. After the award ceremony, a beauty pageant winner and fellow awardee asked me if she could click a photograph with me, as according to her I was a TEDx Speaker.

During my travel when I requested the flight crew for a photograph, all pretty women with lots of makeup posed and tried standing close to me. One of them said with pride that she was flying me the second time and the co-pilot escorted me till the end of the stairs. Minimalism was showing its powers and I could not believe it but the "naked face" made people believe in me more, trust me more-that was clear.

This minimalism life made me more impactful everywhere in a short span of time.

More is Less

In some cases, less is more and in some other cases, more is less.

I often feel what I do is not enough as there is much more I could do.

I had usually seen women speaking of more is less when it came to religious ritualistic acts or housework meaning no matter how much you do is not enough and that it would make you a perfect woman.

I, however, thought of this concept differently.

I enrolled in several courses together, took up multiple projects and collaboration, volunteered for several causes and organization that were under my domain of work. I had lots of discussions and meetups with changemakers just so I could grow myself, develop new perspectives and insights, to become more empathetic and understand the people and the world better.

I wanted to do more good deeds and so I would be on the lookout all day and grab any opportunity that comes. I strived for a balanced day and therefore did a lot of different things and took a quick nap or power nap to get the energy back, if need be. I sometimes treated myself to what I loved eating or to what I loved watching or listening just to freshen up but really very quick and avoiding or suddenly closing it when I feel I can do without it. I did my best to avoid overdoing because that would be an unnecessary distraction that I could not afford.

Occasionally, I ended up being overwhelmed due to the amount of work and focus needed or leading to exhaustion or too many things to tell or ask people both outside and at home, for personal and professional life.

Over time I learned to deal with this and I'm still learning.

I have marked areas and identified things I would do at home, at my workplaces, on the passions I have by refining my role and title so that I could delegate the rest. I started working with intelligent girls and boys who learned quickly and they got my mentorship in return. Those girls and boys were beginners and they enjoyed it.

At home, I usually preferred heavy work that took less time but more brains or energy or other stuff too.

In every place, home or workplace, people may expect or want or force you to contribute more but you must learn to draw the line, to speak up for yourself. Trust me, if your work and intention are noble and efforts are sincere, you will manage to make that happen with God's help.

You must, however, make sure that the sleeping, eating or work habits doesn't become such that it hurts you in the long run thereby hurting others too and affecting your impact.

For example, I would eat at home, earlier than the rest of the family if required for lunch or dinner. There were also times when I was hungry earlier but I avoided so that I could eat with the family and it does not become a habit. We ate lunch and dinner around 1 PM and 7:30 PM respectively. For sleep, I avoided sleeping when something important was happening at home even if I was exhausted. There were times when I would sleep early and take rest so that my productivity increased over the next few days if I saw myself feeling tired or overwhelmed any day.

There were days when I had lots of work but I slept early just so my family would be happy that day but I would do some productive work on sofa or carpet or bed later on, with earphones plugged so that I make myself happy too. It was usually a talk or song or sometimes exercise or very rarely movie or serial.

The weekly to-do list helped as I could do tasks the next day if I could not complete on one day and by the end of the week, I would have done it all. Being human, I sometimes ended up not doing some tasks as per my to-do and timeline either due to laziness or lack of inspiration or fear or double work. For example, the thought of cleaning up the cupboard made me feel lazy if work was at hand or I was tired. I either convinced myself to clean up by listening to motivational talks or songs to inspire me and work at the same time or I did it during weekends when I felt like doing.

I often failed to write my talks ahead of time or when I sent the final topic to the organizers as I didn't feel excited enough to do it ahead of time. I was worried that I would get bored reading it and then bore my audience. That was unacceptable to me. My best talks have happened 1-2 days or hours before the event. That helped me remember the order of the points, saving time and energy otherwise gone in revision and memorizing anything twice.

The last-minute pressure did a lot of good to me during public speaking and so did spontaneous challenges. It helped me give my best, to customize or to innovate to address a problem or challenge.

It gave me time for more important things and so many other things to do. That was possible and worked for me because I read and learnt almost daily. I reflected on daily events too.

Struggles will be there

No matter what choices you make or how well you make them, no matter what you do and how you do it, struggles will always be there.

Perfection, complete peace, no fights and no conflict are impossible even if your intentions are the best and the purest.

Being good does not mean you will have it easy. Being good means you will find it easier each time as you learn and you just have to decide whether it's worth the struggle or not.

You must decide if it's aligned with who you are, what you love and care about, what matters to you in the short and long term. This could be about study, work, relationships and life in general.

Always ask yourself: "What matters more? What will matter more in the years to come?"

That helped me make a lot of decisions and will help you make better decisions. When I thought that way and acted, each time doors started opening, things started falling into place and the clouds of doubts slowly drifted away, allowing light to enter me and my life.

For work, I was mostly doing freelancing which suited me. I wanted to do work I loved and was passionate about but I needed to be financially strong and independent, to learn from the best systems that had been in operation for years as well as innovate and to keep growing myself and building a better me and contributing to a better world. That's what mattered more in the long run.

I eventually started to learn to balance the work types, balance personal and professional life and balance between freelance and "stable work" but always doing the work that I loved.

For causes, if I participated in every cause and event then I realized I won't be able to create long-lasting quality and quantity impact. Social work to me wasn't just doing good deeds but doing it well with what I was good at so that the impact was bigger and deeper.

In the long run, what mattered more was credibility if I practiced what I preached as much as I could, if I genuinely did it without corruption of thoughts or actions if my work influenced the hearts of people or the core of the systems.

Should and Must

I realized that society loved "should" because it was about telling others what to do, how to do and even why they "should" do it. That is how many marketing strategies are planned and the advertisements reflect that.

I understood that "should" in relationships can be very destructive. It is like putting your expectations out there for others to blindly follow, not caring about the people if they want it or not. "Should" is often cruel and hurtful.

To me, it is a very negative word in the way it is used in most places and contexts. It sounds offensive too. I felt that I have not used the word should but have insisted with certain people and messed up big time. I am trying to understand why I did that and fixing it so that a better me can lead to a better India and better World. I will learn to not use or practice "should" in life areas where I could not avoid earlier.

"Must" is different.

Must according to me emphasizes the need and importance of something and that will bring about progress in some form or other. It's like doing or telling someone to do something authentic, true and real, which will lead to a positive situation in some way or the other.

For example, when I tell my elders: "You should not indulge in small talk or worry too much about things that don't matter." I get responses like: "Oh no! She starts again. Who are you to tell us what to do?"

But when I have used the word "must" to say: "You must not worry too much. It will do you no good. You are hurting yourself only." To which I got responses like: "See this girl. We are so blessed. She is right. What is there to worry about. How nicely she explained."

It is kind of funny and strange but "should" has put me in a lot of trouble. "Must" has saved me while giving people the impression that I love and care for them and care for more important things.

Can and Can't

Going through daily struggles in life, at study, work and relationships make us stressed, doubting our abilities and potential sometimes to the extent it makes us doubt ourself and what we can do and who we can be.

You might say: "I can't do it anymore. I feel like giving up." I have said it too.

Saying "I Can't" for things that can change your world and our world will lead to destruction, more hopelessness, more suffering, more heartbreaks and brokenness.

That is why "I Can" is so important.

"I Can" requires a lot of courage, faith in the unseen, belief in God and self, consistent effort and good noble intentions but it does wonders. It does miracles.

"I Can" might have a hint of doubt or lots of it but it's also about putting hope into yourself that you are willing to give it a shot, to start that journey that may not be visible or clear but will lead to something better than the current situation. It gives you the power to start, the motivation to dream and do, to imagine what is possible.

I Will

These two words are loaded with power and potential for miracles.

These words may sound light because of the frequent usage in junior classes or at school.

It wasn't until my life changed when the books I read and the courses I did made me think of "I Will" deeply.

"I Will" makes you own and show up, to act responsibly and force you to not give up, no matter what. It gives out the message that you are not going to settle for less, that what you are aiming for you will have it, that even if you don't deserve it or are not enough qualified but you will make sure you become the deserving with God's help and hard work.

"I Will" puts pressure on you to act urgently, to not waste time, to focus on what matters more, to make you believe in you and make others believe in you.

Using "I Will" in the positive self-talk is very critical and significant to have a good relationship with God and yourself.

GIG is what matters more

Looking at the last few years when I have seen success and failure differently, I realized what led to who I am today and what is crucial for becoming who I want to be is GIG- God. Intentions. Grind.

For any aspect of my life, GIG worked and is working.

I strive to put God first, what He wants is for you to live a life of purpose and what is good for you and humanity. After that, I keep renewing and repeating my intentions while working hard and doing my best each day.

Reflection is very important as it helps me do better the next time, to help me live a better tomorrow than today, reducing guilt, mistakes, loss of time and energy each time so that I could learn more, do more and be more.

A junior from my high school at the gym once told me about a song, "Aashayein" and the words: "Kuch aisa karke dikha, khud khush ho jaye khuda" which roughly translates to "to do something that God becomes really happy" (and does miracles for you.) These words encourage me to do "things beyond normal," to do things in such a way that God might be so happy with me that He will create miracles for me.

Miracles happen every day.

Each of us witnesses it inside us and outside. But to receive miracles that transforms both, you cannot do what everybody does or do it the way everyone does.

The intentions, sacrifice, method and ethics have to be such that most people would give up on but if you persist then miracles will be sent your way!

Stage and Soil

When it comes to impact, most people either prefer the stage to show their success and greatness or they prefer the soil for the same reasons. I, however, feel a need for balance in both.

The work on the ground, on the soil, must be very thorough and thoughtfully done so that you are deserving of the stage, so that you really inspire and positively influence when on the stage, when your experiences on soil keeps you grounded and empathetic to serve your people, your country and God the best way possible.

The stage, titles and recognition are not bad, they could act as catalysts, giving more encouragement and confidence to the one receiving it and those who know about it. It gives the person more platforms to increase the impact and increases their reach among people to reach out to those who really need it.

The soil is important too as that is the laboratory for learning, creating, testing while being open-minded, empathetic, curious and compassionate.

REFLECT:

1. In which areas of your life will the "more" be applicable and in which areas will "less" be applicable? Elaborate on each and share your why.

2. After reading this chapter on "Inspiration 9," what new insights have you developed on more and less, more is less and less is more?

X

Going and Growing through it

I never wanted to study Botany as my choice of subject was Zoology. Studying Botany, however, is one of the best things that has happened to me. A lot of people consider it a waste if you don't study your bachelors subject till Ph.D. or make a career out of it.

I was able to build myself and my life, the real life out of this experience of studying pure science in high school, botany in bachelors and later teacher training and self-learning.

I was blessed with the best teacher and mentor any person could have- Dr. Illora Sen. Her classes and lessons were about Botany but made me reflect on life too.

Lessons from Botany classes

I remember studying algae and fungi in the first year when I came across the words "unfavourable conditions" for the growth of a plant. In life, all of us have unfavourable conditions that make us feel uncomfortable, scared, nervous and hopeless. What I learned from plants is to thrive in unfavourable conditions by adaptation.

The ultimate goal has to be accomplished.

The big picture has to be kept in mind.

There are plants that will die but there are those that will continue to grow and thrive. Giving up isn't a choice at all.

It's interesting how xerophytic plants function, to deal with the unfavourable conditions. They inspire me to "have roots that are strong and deep, to extract nutrition and inspiration in the deep and dark."

Situations will never be perfect and struggles will always be there. I learned to stretch myself through learning and prayer and get nutrition and inspiration for my soul and the world around, to deal with the struggles.

I love nights and darkness because it helps me to look within and above, and talk to God. There are times I have cried for almost all day or for few hours or days, trying to hold back tears amidst people but at the same time try to learn something from that experience so that I feel empowered.

Darkness makes me stronger as I critically analyze myself, to look at my weaknesses and feel the need to improve and change for the better. There is no reason to not like darkness as it is going to be a part of my day and part of my life on Earth. It will help if I learn to accept it and create a system to deal with it productively so that it won't scare me forever.

Cactus develops a different form of stem characteristics to deal with extremes which inspires me to sometimes develop and put on an appearance that reflects my indifference to a situation or sometimes my ignoring it due to lack of its importance in my life. It may be bothering me a lot but I learned "to fake till I make it." When you give something too much thought and time, it dominates the thinking process and affects your daily life a lot which makes you unproductive and your day unproductive too.

At times I knew why people called me and what the conversation was going to be about. If I felt it would bother me or make my mood bad and whole day unproductive then I ignored it and focused on what was more important. In case the conversation was needed then I tried to have it at night so that I could cry myself to sleep or talk to God peacefully. I would wake up all energized to fight harder and better the next day.

I learned that amidst the unfavourable conditions, I couldn't just sit back for light to show up or for something favourable to happen. It must come from within and the initiative has to be taken, the courage gathered.

I believe it's important to take risks after reasoning why you are taking it, weighing advantages and disadvantages in light of what's good for you and humanity, whether your decision or action will, in the end, bring glory to humanity, make God happy and result in your soul being at peace and content. If this is clear then, by all means, take the risk because you won't know what can happen till you take it and see it through.

Maybe you will have a happier life, you will have more to offer to the people and the world and see your impact spreading far and wide, everywhere. Maybe all the people who are upset today with you or hurt will see the light and also be happy and proud of you. Maybe everything you ever wanted is on the other side and you will have it all even if it seems impossible now. You won't know till you take the risk.

God rewards very heavily with miracles, those that take risks to serve the people and to make the world a better place. The results may not show up immediately, it might occur slowly but surely you will see the unexpected and get the reward. That is His Promise and how He blessed the great people in the past and He will do to you as well. "Believe and don't give up yet," I would tell myself.

One of the things I learned from Robin Sharma and others is the significance of affirmations.

What others tell you is not as important as what you tell yourself.

The words you tell yourself, the conversation you have with yourself decides whether you will make the world better or bitter.

In the end, people withdraw and distance themselves and you have to face yourself and God so make sure you have the right conversation at the right time with yourself and God.

The rest of the world and your loved ones will adjust and understand when you are successful or leave that to God completely.

If they do not understand or adjust then you don't need to worry as according to me, in the end, it's between you and God. I serve others for God so after doing my best if they are not happy then I have done my part. I often tell myself: "Madiha, you have made it so far. But there is more. More places to go. More lives to change. More mountains to climb and conquer. God made you. He created you. You owe it to Him and no one else. You have to be true to Him and yourself even if others distrust you or doubt you."

Solid Roots

I recall studying poems in class 10 for my board exams that were on life and the importance of not bending to struggles in life. There are motivational songs that talk about the need for God otherwise a person will be chasing every wind that blows his or her way or bending to every pressure from around.

I realized the importance of roots while studying photosynthesis.

When the roots are healthy, strong and deep, water and nutrients can be absorbed well and transported upwards to all parts of the plant leading to a healthy plant that "bears fruits."

Similarly, in life, roots are the values and principles that I must hold onto and never give up on, to have a system in place to deal with fear, failure and mistakes so that the comeback is stronger and my soul is efficiently striving for more important things always.

I developed a mechanism and system to deal with fear by asking myself: "What's the worst thing that can happen?"

People will criticize? That they will do irrespective of whether you do the wrong or right thing.

You will be alone? You came into this world alone and you will go back alone.

You will die? In the end, everyone leaves this world. It is not the number of years but the quality of years you have lived that matters. If I have lived well then death at any point doesn't scare me.

To deal with failure, I keep saying to myself and others: "I am a human. There are things I don't know and I have not experienced yet and maybe never will. I don't know a lot of things. But I'm a learner. I do make mistakes but ask for feedback to improve, to learn more and do better."

To deal with mistakes, I reflect on what goes wrong like checking a Math sum. I go through the incident step by step and in order and then figure out which part or step I could improve on and how. I look up resources and call out for help, I learn from experts if required so that I can serve others better when I am focused on being better.

In my interactions, I try to talk and sit, walk, learn and discuss with the rich and the poor, the educated and the ignorant. That helps to keep me humble. My lifestyle as described in previous chapters also helped to bring stability to my life as I grow as do the causes I believe in and work for positive growth.

Light and Reflection

If your dreams are big then your struggles will also be big.

That is why it's important to have clarity about light, your source of inspiration, who you can go back to, someone much bigger and powerful than the world, its creations and its creatures put together. Since class 8, I became more alert and aware of this aspect of my life.

During my train journey, I made a deal as a teenager with God that if I followed my conscience, His way and do what He wants me to do for the greater good then He will give me success and everything I want. Since then, over the years, I have realized I have gone back to Him, time and again, knowing full well that He is the One I can trust and rely on for all my needs and wants. He is the One who listens and never misunderstands or misinterprets me and my intentions.

He is the One who has heard me and been there for me during the darkest and the toughest moments. I can tell Him anything anytime and I get the answers through different ways from Him- sometimes through peace in the heart or mind, sometimes people I trust saying something or someone totally unexpected saying something or something unexpected or expected happening, incidents or events around me. Sometimes it is the weather, words or quotes sent by people or appearing in my newsfeed.

The source of light in my life is God. I love Him because He has not given up on me, He has inspired me even during times when I was feeling low or lazy. I was able to fight both and still do most of the time. Those two years in the past changed the way I looked at religion, spirituality and faith.

Reflection is the key to a great life, a life of alertness, constantly improving, with better actions and greater impact. During my talk at a national conference as I previously mentioned, I spoke on "Re-Search the Soul." I have been practicing reflection since I was a teenager.

While studying electrons and protons, I felt that electrons were like selfish people who only took things from others and became negative whereas protons were like selfless or generous people who gave things to others and became positive.

From photosynthesis, I understood more about social change as described earlier in this book too. When the light rays strike the internally situated chlorophyll only then food is produced and not when it strikes the superficial epidermal layers.

In life, if we want to bring change then light and inspiration have to strike the heart and transform it. Only then will that transformed heart create transformed individuals, as well as society, like the plant where food from one part is then circulated to other parts.

If science is not accompanied by reflection then there will be more destruction and damage than blessings.

Growth and Pain

I remember teaching the life cycle of a butterfly to orphanage kids and see the wonder on their faces. We also discussed what would happen if the cocoon was removed by us and not naturally. I recalled reading a story of a boy who tried to help the butterfly come out of the cocoon and how it dies very soon. The butterfly needs to undergo the pain and struggle to come out of the cocoon so that it becomes stronger.

Growth and greatness require pain.

Here are a few reflections on them:

-You must avoid unnecessary pain at all costs about things that you might want or desire and not need, things not so beneficial in the long run or in the big picture.

Pain can be really exhausting. It will consume your precious energy, time and thought process and that's why it's important to go through pain for things that matter more and lead to positive growth for yourself and people around you.

-There will be things and circumstances that will be unavoidable and cause you pain. In many cases, the pain can be reduced by not thinking too much or not being too aware of the situation.

When it happens to me, I think of good and happy things, do activities to keep me engaged so that my mind doesn't divert in that direction. Sometimes I slept through pain and used the time to rest and relax when otherwise I had less time to do either.

Even today, there are times when I am awake and feeling the pain, using the time to reflect and do my best work, develop great and deep insights on life or just to clean up my email or phone.

-I believe moments of pain and struggles give out a lot of information which if processed can lead to transformation. I have used this powerful technique over the last 8-9 years to strengthen me, to develop a shield around my heart to prevent it from extreme heartbreak and betrayal, to understand people and relationships.

For example, in a relationship, the usage of certain words, the frequency of usage of words or length or quality of conversation creates problem or misunderstanding. Different people deal with words differently. I realized that in my interactions with near and dear ones that all of them are not happy with words. This is because their love language, how they express love and how they like love to be expressed, is different from mine mostly.

During my recruit process, I came across a quiz based on a book in 5-6 love languages. Jay Shetty, a motivational speaker also shared this on his YouTube channel.

Most of us treat others and express love to our loved ones in our love language rather than theirs.

Processing the information after going through a painful experience will help you grow and bring about transformation.

-Transformation and just the thought of it might scare a lot of people as it requires a mind-shift, a big change. It requires going beyond and above what you are used to in your daily life. But once you take that first step and choose to bear the pain, to go through the struggle then things become easier and you start developing tools and a system to deal with it effectively.

Celebrating small successes during the "painful" transformation journey might act as a boost, encouragement and push you to go further, to not quit and make things happen.

The grass is greener on the other side?!

When you see others successful or happy, you might think the grass is greener on their side.

Sometimes it leads to jealousy, bitterness, destruction mode and sometimes gossip and backbiting. It's great to admire the green grass on the other side and give words of encouragement.

It's better if you use that to inspire yourself to grow your own grass and to grind to keep it green, to grow your plants and trees, to see your fruits grow.

Watching and wishing will not lead to growth and transformation in your life.

Wishing for the same as the other side has, might make you unhappy. I believe in "growing grass, plants and trees" based on my liking and interests, making my garden unique and beautiful.

The life others lead, the choices others make, the places they go, the things they buy, the people they meet, the work they do, what and where they hang out, the entertainment, fun and food they have access to and they enjoy, might make you dream and wish for the same or give out the impression that those people have it easy. I believe no one has it easy.

It's our own attitude, beliefs and actions that will help us deal with pain and struggles, to overcome them.

Your struggles and my struggles may be the same or different, different in levels, in different phases but that does not mean either of us has it easy.

It's just that either of us has learned to deal with it effectively, to stop allowing it to dominate our systems greatly or deeply.

Self-learning

This involves two things- firstly being a self-made person and secondly learning about oneself.

After my formal education as a student of B.Sc Botany, I took a 4 year break to learn and explore multiple things from diverse sources and fields to increase my knowledge, to explore the different technologies and topics that exist or that people talk about, to be creative and find like-minded people to learn and work with. I came across OpenIDEO through an email sent by

Colonel Prabir Sengupta. I loved the open innovation platform where people and ideas connected, where people contributed to and built each other's ideas, collaborated on solutions for some of the most pressing problems faced by the people in different countries.

I learned more about myself and others through learning and applying what I learned in my daily life. Being a self-made person and learning about yourself is related and they happen simultaneously most of the time. Here are a few reflections on them:

Forget them, remember you

Due to life challenges and the people around, you may often think about those people, the society, what will they think, what will they say and so on. This kind of thinking may dominate you so much that you may forget you, you may forget what you think, what you need and want. This is not good for you or for humanity.

Forget about the words they said and actions they did to hurt you or destroy you or criticise you. Revenge will not help. Thinking constantly about it won't help. It won't heal either. There was a time when people were criticising me or hurting me, even calling up my folks "out of concern" to tell them "I needed to slow down or stop."

There was a time when I gave them a lot of thought, fighting and arguing with them in my head, planning rarely that I would get back in some way or the other. But while preparing for my workshop on past, I realized they did not deserve so much space in my head or heart and time and that too for negative reasons. I feared ending up being a vessel full of negativity that would not only be a danger to humanity but my own self too.

I knew I was standing up against society because it was incapable of standing up for itself and for its own good.

I love people in general, leading them, working with them, seeing them happy and I wanted the same for more and more people.

A leader has to be working with people but have a higher vision to take them higher.

I started to forget them, their negative contributions more and more, starting to focus on solutions and creating something new so that old systems and beliefs start becoming obsolete. But this was a huge challenge as it required to have the best resources and knowledge of the old cultural and religious beliefs and practices, that of the new and latest innovative practices and ideas backed by proper research.

I realized that the past few years from 18-21 years of my age I took a keen interest in religion and spirituality, to study it and therefore insights that I developed, the intellect, heart and soul I had now, saw spirituality and religion very differently. Since 22 years of age, due to events and social work, I was learning and researching the latest innovative beliefs and practices in the field of spirituality all over the world.

I was beginning to discuss, argue, to fight my battles and for humanity for which I was called rude and disrespectful too but every single person I could see was taken aback often by the logic and reacted with hurt or tears in their eyes and words. They wondered how this "sweet, polite, respectful" girl had become "such."

I forgot about them. I remembered myself and humanity, the big picture. It was important for me to be a self-made person, not a society-made person because years down the line and maybe on my deathbed or during my illnesses at any time when I could be bedridden, I do not want to feel regret for not listening to my heart but listening to too many confusing and contradictory noises and words.

I knew that those who were society-made felt happy rather faked it really well a lot of times only to have a terrible time during illness or old age because of their mind and conscience not allowing them the peace they wanted.

Society-made people may please everybody but they miss out on the blessing of pleasing God and receiving and witnessing miracles. They may see success and have it all but miss out on satisfaction.

I had seen too many society-made people and thus I decided I would be a self-made person with the help of God so that I would have lesser expectations to live up to, lesser guilt and heartbreak due to others. I wanted to be a self-made person who lived her life to the fullest and learned from her mistakes each day.

Build the person you want to be

A lot of people say this: "I can't be this because my family or spouse won't allow me to be!"

When I was faced with this challenge, I started looking inside, exploring and analyzing myself.

I realized I felt that way because honestly, I didn't know what I really wanted and why. Due to the lack of clarity on my own part, I had no courage or confidence to stand up for what I wanted and who I wanted to be.

A lot of times you may think: "You know what you want but can't have it." When I was able to figure out "what I didn't want" and not yet clear about "what I wanted," I imagined myself in action a few minutes, hours, days, weeks, months, years from now. I analyzed how I felt thinking and acting in that imaginary situation.

I would ask myself: "If not this then what do you want to be or do?"

It was like trying on clothes sometimes, how I would like a certain scene in my head and sometimes not, the difference was clothes and fashion were not the most important things that time but they gave me hints on the role I could play in different scenes to make important decisions.

I sometimes saw photographs and profiles of successful women and men and got ideas, gradually learning about what I wanted and what I didn't want.

Building the person you want to be is a lot about leading yourself like you would lead others or a company- planning carefully, paying attention to minute details, managing every aspect of it, doing critical feedback- rewarding and having accountability based on analysis, constantly growing and branding well.

Many people don't take personal branding seriously due to various reasons. Even I didn't for a long time. I started becoming aware and conscious, serious and focused on it due to my close friends.

I realized that if I wasn't doing it consciously then the world will do it for me. I learned more about personal branding, got my logo and website ready with the help of my scientist friend, Mr. Jawwad Patel's feedback. He suggested .org for my website.

By being conscious, planning well, reflecting each day, staying updated in terms of knowledge in personal and professional life, interacting with diverse group of people globally, thinking only of the best, striving to say and do the best, I was learning about who I wanted to be and gradually acquiring the tools, resources and networks to build that me that I wanted to be. It was a lot of hard work no doubt but totally worth it.

There were times I felt like not doing something but I would tell myself: "Madiha, you only have one chance at this life, to create legacy, to build a "me" that would leave behind a legacy and live a life that I was proud of and that having lived, I could stand before God, completely worn out, used and content to be able to say: "God, I did everything I could with your help."

As I undertook my journey at 23, I started feeling a strong desire to help others and to help them build themselves so that we could all contribute to building a Peaceful World for all and for generations to come.

Mindfulness and Mindful Disruption

Sometimes you may think: "It's okay to have fun, to do things once in a while or when you are young."

You may think, say, do things as they occur to you based on the internal processing of observations, memories and desires or based on external factors or pressure. This leads to an average life, many a time an unproductive life, a life you may regret later.

The regret could be because of not doing "what you could have done" or because "you listened to others and got carried away."

Mindfulness requires you to understand how you think and feel, when and why and how that happens, to be alert and constantly analyzing. It isn't easy at all but once you start accepting and living this way, it becomes the normal act gradually, less exhausting and overwhelming.

Having said that I have never been 100% successful but more than 80% successful where I now choose to shut off a certain thought process by doing something that I know will keep me deeply engaged. It's possible only when I want to.

Mindfulness needs determination which will come with the clarity of purpose. When I recall my purpose, I get back the energy to work harder and focus on what's more important. I am then able to practice mindfulness and stop myself from thinking, saying and acting in a certain way even if I was close to accomplishing it or stop while in the process.

Mindfulness is powerful in transforming your life and the world around you. It also gives me the opportunity and makes me on the receiving end of miracles because I do it through "good deeds for the sake of God" and ask for something really big when in dire need of it, when all doors seem to be closed, when I feel like I have no control over me or things either due to the magnitude of the situation or my human feelings and behaviour.

Mindful Disruption is when you mindfully break out of or shatter, reject or rebel against certain beliefs and practices with a purpose and while being conscious, doing it while analyzing in order to be effective and impactful.

Our countries, our cities, our communities, our homes, our own souls need mindful disruption for a better and peaceful world for all.

That, of course, starts with the individual which then is powerful to influence other levels.

I started practicing mindful disruption two years back when I heard something from society and it didn't feel right or just. I started analyzing the situation, I would try to read up news or articles on those topics or issues followed by processing the information, listing advantages and disadvantages, positives and negatives and then again thinking or imagining about the situation in a more personal way to understand if it felt right and just, if it didn't prick my conscience, if I could hold a logical and honest conversation in my head with people who mattered and felt there was clarity. It is then I would know what to do or how to go about a certain thing.

In case after all these steps and carefulness, if I ended up making a mistake or with different results that I am not happy with, then I process where and what went right, identify areas of improvement on my own or with the feedback of trusted people, virtual or in-person but virtual mostly- from people I knew and from experts or speakers I trusted, my mentors!

REFLECT:

1. Recall some of the toughest moments of your life when you felt like giving up, when you saw no hope and no way ahead. How do you feel about them today? What helped you grow and become the person you are today? Are you happy with the person you are?

2. What action will you take after reading this chapter on "Inspiration 10" to deal with the pain and struggles in your life?

XI

Dilemma of the Rich, Humble, Passionate and Generous

One of the most important things I've learned in this journey of life is that we all yearn for a rich life- richness in a materialistic and spiritualistic way.

I have seen this yearning in the young and the old, the rich and the poor, the educated and the uneducated.

This yearning is not geography-specific, background-specific, gender-specific, culture-specific, religion-specific.

It's just something every soul desires.

There is the richness of the soul and the richness of the sole where the sole represents materialistic things while the soul represents something deeper and more meaningful. Some of us yearn for the materialistic richness of the sole and there are some of us who yearn for the richness of the soul. Some yearn for both.

The two kinds of Richness

I belong to this category of an individual yearning for both the richness of soul and sole.

When the soul is rich, the richness of sole gets attracted to you as well, as I started to experience it in my life. My own family background and ancestors had both and therefore the desire came to me but I wanted the richness to go to the next level and have my unique touch to it, to create a legacy "in spite of being a girl" and not "carrying the name" forward and doing it my way.

I was thinking about the differences between the richness of the sole and the soul and this is what I came up with:

a) Richness of the sole can be robbed. Richness of the soul cannot be robbed.

b) Richness of the sole is difficult to share while that of the soul is easy to share.

c) Richness of the sole brings envy that is bad but that associated with the soul is good if it helps compete to do more good.

d) Richness of the sole could be temporary but that of the soul can be eternal.

I definitely wanted more richness of soul than the richness of the sole as the majority wanted the opposite, which sometimes led to terrible consequences for the self and humanity if acquired through the wrong means.

I definitely wanted the richness of sole to be able to do more courses, travel and attend events, start and sustain a social enterprise, to fulfill hidden dreams of my elders. I needed it to be able to contribute to the family (existing and new) and be a partner in growth and progress for the family, to give surprises to my loved ones.

Measuring Richness

It's important that we are able to measure what we have and the impact it creates.

The richness of sole is easier to measure through bank balance, charity receipts, travel tickets, forms and paperwork. I wondered how richness of soul could be measured and if there were any indicators for it.

I believe one of the best indicators of the richness of soul is good character.

What had always amazed me how people spoke of good and bad character and declared someone as possessing good or bad character. The declaration did not seem to have a sound basis which is what bothered me for a long time.

We humans may act or speak, make big decisions without really understanding the consequences.

Society's definition of good character wasn't acceptable to me because of my past and present experiences. Those men or families who were known to possess "good character" acted most unjustly and had traits that made me rethink the definition of "educated," "modern" and "religious."

Think of a person who is well-settled, having a great relationship with parents but objecting to a woman's choice of covering her head.

Looking back at my own life and the criticism I went through where my character was being questioned, I was surprised at those elders who objected to my interaction with men. These were men who were themselves "very free" with other women, interacted a great deal with lots of women. These were females who shook hands with men or even a hug from "some." These were people who broke religious rules and then so boldly and shamelessly questioned me. I wonder at the "religious female" who preached religion, modesty and gender interaction to me, created such unnecessary conflicts when "her own" sons during their study abroad posted shameless photographs with females. I do stalk people if needed to bring out the truth.

I am doing my research on character building education to share it with the world.

Society's perception of a good character

It's when a person does no wrong in public, does not stand up or speak up against their practices, the evils they indulge in with the sugar coating of "we care" or "we have seen more of the world than you" and so on.

It is when a person pleases people and wants to stay in their good books at all costs or as much as possible.

It is when a person obeys anything and everything elders or society says without processing or questioning internally or externally or even if their heart says otherwise, even if they have to suffer all their life, be miserable and causes more harm than good in the big picture.

For society, good character is associated with silence at the cost of inner turmoil which could lead to depression, suicidal tendencies, drugs, unethical sex and playing with others lives. It is associated with superficial appearance and perfection at the cost of complete brokenness, struggling to breathe or witness even one moment of peace.

To keep up the image of a good character, more evil and corrupt practices may be acceptable, more crimes may be committed, more damage may be done than good, more secrecy and plotting, more and more pretense adopted.

It broke my heart to see such unnecessary suffering among people that could be avoided. I was feeling the pain watching and hearing the way people spoke and how they behaved, the pain on their faces, in their words and actions not aligned with words. I was under pressure since early days, at school, home or workplace to give in to this attitude, this mindset, this framework and system just to be called someone with a good character belonging to a noble and good family.

This is what society thinks: "Good girls and boys from good families don't speak up, they obey and adjust, they "refrain" (refrain actually from good things that are good for self or humanity?)."

It was only at 23 that I got the courage and wisdom to see the reality, to stand up and speak up against it. I stopped worrying about what people thought because I knew pleasing people would bring no benefits, they might change their attitude, they may start speaking ill of me behind my back when at one time they would have loved or praised you.

It wasn't worth pleasing people so I knew pleasing God was the best thing, fighting with His People for His People and for His Sake because they didn't know what was good for them. In some cases after years of "seeing the world" and "having seen more of it."

I learned from my own experiences that pleasing God brought more miracles in this sometimes complicated and somewhat evil world which can be very overwhelming and contradictory.

To serve humanity and transform lives, I needed God and only God could help me, as with Him, transparency was possible.

I knew that so far I witnessed miracles because God knew the real picture even if the people painted it differently and they accused, criticized or questioned me.

I was always questioned because I asked too many questions or because I believed in transparency, being raw and real and really wanted and stood up for understanding things and people.

Due to lack of exposure and seeing limited things and the reality of the world due to over-protection, lack of awareness of things that mattered and things that must have been spoken about rather than hushed, I, like a lot of youth and elders, had for some time fallen into the trap of society.

Society is strange as a lot of times it will create a trap, create criminals and then punish them. It will then cry that the world is a bad place and put up their own definition of good character, of who an educated, modern, wise or religious person is.

My thoughts on good character

In my opinion, good character is much more than sweet words and actions that please everyone and that are done in accordance with the majority, powerful, elders. It is more than just keeping everyone happy and obeying them. According to me, good character is associated with:

a) Mindfulness and striving to be a mindful disruptor in personal and public spaces.

b) Being a Striving soul rather than a perfect one because the latter can't exist. It is not possible to have a single negative or unproductive thought or action in a day. Why fake perfection when it doesn't exist?

A striving soul is one which is fighting every time with itself to stay authentic to itself and God, sometimes successful and sometimes unsuccessful.

When it's unsuccessful, it strives to accept and identify its mistakes, learn and do better, to say sorry to those concerned and wronged and to God, without brooding and feeling sorry for too long to move in the direction of betterment, hope and growth.

A striving soul acknowledges its own shortcomings, others contributions but at the end holding itself accountable to make better and informed choices and decisions.

A striving soul promises itself to stay raw and real and true to itself and God.

One of the ways I have found through experiences to stay a striving soul is to take each day at a time for accountability. At the end of the day, I went through the entire day either with the help of my to-do list or through a mental screening of events. This is to identify what went right and be happy about it, thank God for it and to identify what I could make better so that my tomorrow is better than today.

I follow the 3 R's- "Reduce, Replace, Reflect" methodology which I shared during one of my workshops too.

Step 1: Reduce is when you decrease the frequency or magnitude of a thought, words or action.

For example, you might be eating a lot of sweets and therefore putting on weight so you try to reduce the frequency which means the number of times you consume sweets in a day or week or reduce the quantity, meaning the number of sweets each time or the quantity of sugar in the dessert.

Step 2: Replace is when you substitute a negative, unhealthy or unproductive option with a positive, healthy or productive one, partially or completely.

For example, if you normally watch videos every time it is sent to you or read every message forwarded to you from everyone then you must replace that habit with videos or messages at a particular time of the day or week and just forget about those you couldn't watch or read. Prioritization of videos and messages can be done on the basis of the credibility of the people sending it or depending on what mood you are in.

If you have been serious for too long and feel exhausted and you like funny things then read or watch funny things. If you are a person who jokes normally then you might want to go for something that is a bit serious. In case of food and desserts more specifically because I have a sweet tooth, I replace them with fruits so that the desire for sweet is fulfilled partly with healthy options.

Step 3: Reflect is when you introspect and look within and outside on what you did well and what you could improve on the next day. Based on that you could repeat Reduce and Replace steps.

Reflection helps you to identify areas or people, places, events, words that trigger or influence the thought process and actions.

c) Another thing associated with a good character according to me is restraint which is developed through prayer, reflection, mindfulness, acting spontaneously, company of people, hobbies and places you hang out.

It is indeed important to be raw and real but there is also the need for a checking system called restraint that you do not give in to every desire and then end up regretting, feeling guilty and depressed for a long time and then overcoming those for some more time.

Once two married females friends were discussing if they saw a hot guy would they give in to their desires or restraint? Both said they would give in. Then they asked me and I said: "Restraint." They inquired if it was because I was a Muslim, if my religion stopped me or my culture did. I said: "Sex to me is sacred. How can you end up doing with anyone? Also, sex is something that society might emphasize a man must enjoy alone or lead. I believe that both the woman and the man must enjoy and take turns to lead. Safety plays a key role here. Unless I feel safe with someone, I trust someone fully and have a mental connection with, pleasure won't be mutual. Outside the bond of marriage, there is a lack of safety and trust and it's not official."

It's important to really consider this carefully and to think of this sacred act with someone you can connect with. There are those who talk of relationships of other forms, I respect them but I do believe in the sacredness of marriage and that its foundation must be solid, with clarity, with no hide and seek games, and both the man and woman aware of, and understanding what it would lead to.

The current entertainment industry, as well as the past traditional and cultural practices, have made life difficult, giving wrong ideas of love and marriage, of relationships, of loyalty and of ethics.

There are very few role models for the youth to emulate which is why marriages are breaking, that there is a lack of loyalty and peace in marriages. A lot of focused youth get trapped into societal pressure and settle for less which results in the world missing out on good role models in this aspect of life.

In this incident and conversation, I realized there was the element of being raw and real, transparent, of being logical and mindful. It reflected the places and people I hang out with, where this confidence and courage came from- prayers and reflection. Also, the kind of hobbies and activities I indulged in reflected in the thought process. This gave me satisfaction and peace that I was doing what is good for me and for humanity.

Richness and humility, passion, generosity

When it comes to richness, there is often this confusion between humility and pride, between being passionate and calm and practical, between generosity and thinking for yourself.

This dilemma is often due to society's pressure on "good character" which revolves around the extremity of either thinking only of yourself or the other extreme of thinking only of others.

Humility and Pride

Richness is often associated with pride. Sometimes richness of sole is associated with pride and richness of soul associated with humility.

Humility may be seen in the form of suppression of voice and suppression of a person's concerns, giving up easily and obeying seniority in age or power.

Society sometimes forces you to believe that humility lies in keeping quiet, not speaking up or standing up against something that is wrong or evil in the big picture.

In my own experience, humility is when you can convey your message firmly but be polite in language as much as possible but if the other party is bent on doing damage to more people or in the big picture then the voice may be raised while making arguments stronger, intentions more powerful and grind harder. To follow up with some concerned acts and kindness acts after this session of firmness.

Humility is when you are confident in your skin, confident due to a clarity of purpose and therefore sometimes take a step back in things that don't matter more, without fear or hesitancy. It is when you admit the possibility of being wrong and willing to learn when you are sure you have done your homework but things didn't happen as you planned or when you understand something better could be acquired and learned too.

Pride may be seen in the dominance and forceful attitude by society to have its way, to force individuals to be all of the same kind like "factory wholesale production" in accordance to its whims and desires, what is right and wrong according to society, what is pleasing to society irrespective of ethics and the greater good.

It prevents an individual from having healthy self-pride, healthy pride in the community, culture and the country.

Society's idea of pride in the self could result in being authoritative and preventing individuals from having their and others basic rights and basic needs met.

Society's idea of pride in the community could prevent individuals from having a happy and fulfilling life, to follow norms and give in to expectations in spite of all the misery it will bring to all.

Society's idea of pride in the country prevents people from living a dignified life, from serving country in the best, noblest and highest way that's possible. It prevents people from being true assets to the country and humanity in general.

According to me, self-pride is when you know who you are and what you deserve, it is when you refuse to settle for little, when you stand up for yourself because you understand it's also standing up for humanity.

Self-pride is when you admit mistakes and start the journey of reformation and betterment but don't allow yourself to be disrespected. It is when you stand up against injustices done to you and to others.

Pride for the community is when you know the strengths and assets of your community but don't use it or indulge in pulling others down or for mocking other communities or developing a superiority complex. It is when you use this pride to bond well and lift up other communities, be willing to learn from the best in other communities, to improve your own.

Pride in country is when you love your country irrespective of its state and level of greatness and believe in being a dignified citizen, thinking, speaking and acting for its well-being and of its people. It is when you love it so much that you share its best with the world and bring the best of the world to it. It is when you strive to continue the legacy of its past and take things to the next level.

It's alright to be proud of yourself, who you are and speak about it as you have invested in your life through time, intentions and efforts.

It is very important that during self-talk you criticize as well as praise yourself to help you maintain yourself as a balanced person.

Passionate and Being Calm and Practical

Richness is associated with being very passionate about things because anything is possible apparently for someone who is rich, wealthy, resourceful.

Many a time people with the richness of soul have been called "emotional," passionate and not being practical, as people who think, see and act with faith, sacrificing passion and acting too pious and being old fashioned.

People with the richness of sole have been called too passionate, acting irrationally, giving in to their feelings without thinking of the big picture or ethics, acting on impulse without being practical.

From my observation of a lot of people, I felt that passion was associated with being emotional, irrational and impractical leading to guilt and being calm and practical meant that you could not be enthusiastic about the task or situation, you had to be serious, very critical, unemotional to make good decisions.

I found both to be extreme and not leading to success and happiness in the long run.

According to me, passion is when you listen to your heart and "listen to the vibes and feel it," to allow yourself to believe that your heart can be right about things as well.

Many a time my heart has shown me the right path while sometimes listening to it has led to trouble too.

In the past around 23 years of age, a lot of decisions I have been making have been better than I did before.

By better I mean they were informed choices, they were made with the help of people I trusted the most and closest to me. They used to criticize me a lot as well as appreciate a lot in a great way out of concern in the past that hurt me little or sometimes a lot. But I knew that I could trust these people to criticize me if I was wrong or messing up.

Passion is a great trait and you should not fear to have it or acting on it.

When I was faced with the dilemma of yes or no for marriage proposals, I would imagine the best and the worst situation, analyze the reason behind saying yes or no to someone.

I would then let myself be passionate about both my dreams and the possibility of a future with someone I wanted to give a chance to or have a chance with. I mostly ended up more excited about my dreams!

Sometimes you may get very excited about dreams or spouse of dreams and that is human but it's also important you do something to keep you grounded and to keep you practical as well to remind you of the big picture.

I brought the balance through sometimes sharing bits of my plans and ideas with people I trusted, sometimes with strangers as a case study or situation, listening to and watching productive videos of songs or talks that would give me new perspectives and insights.

I heard things that were soft and loud in music or in the motivational talks so that I could feel both ways. When I felt passion level was rising, I worked out or went for a walk to get my energy out and think at the same time or after.

All of this helped me to maintain a moderate level of passion while helping me think clearly, to act with rationality and consciousness too.

Generosity and Thinking for Yourself

The richness of the soul is associated with being generous, giving without expectations of returns, doing everything for "free" while the richness of sole is associated with thinking for yourself, being selfish, thinking about gains for yourself and no one else or nothing else.

Generosity in my experience is about giving and contributing time and money, giving through thoughts, words and actions too.

It is when I wanted to take out some time from my day to think of some genuine friend, do some work for them or counsel them. It's when I choose to stand up and let a poor person who might appear shabby sit in my place in the bus while I stand. It is when I plan the best way possible for the schools or orphanage for impact. There are times when I don't have excess or enough to give to charity in cash but when I do, I buy things and give beggars.

All organizations and people don't need to be given monetary help as it could make them more dependent or corrupted. When a beggar approaches me, I either give food I have like a packet of biscuit or an exercise book or pencil.

I realized helping any person due to pity the way society does, would cripple them. In my opinion, if you really love and care for any person then give them the tools or mentoring or be a listener or facilitator, give them work or anything that will help get work or start work.

Thinking for yourself according to me is about thinking big for yourself and humanity, to talk and act big. It is about remembering that when you preserve yourself, achieve for yourself while not giving up, if you persist in striving to give good a chance and to make good win then you are thinking of and for yourself and for the good and progress of the country as well as humanity at large.

About the Richness of Sole

This is an age where brands matter a lot to people and branding matters which is why people and companies invest in it. On one hand, there are those who can afford and stay loyal to the big names and brands. While those who cannot afford often buy the fake goods sold on streets, of poor quality even just to have the logo of the big brands on themselves, ready to bear the pain that the shoe bite causes, the heat and itching on the body due to the poor quality of materials or the finishing.

I recall going to a luxury mall where I passed different shops and saw prices of very simple goods starting from INR 25k. At one point I was a teenager that yearned for such things but I'm blessed that God taught me early on what matters more. He gave me and gives me success and miracles when I focus more on what matters more.

Once I was returning home with my mom after buying a wrist watch for myself from a Sonata shop and I told her about watches in general: "I wonder if people value the time these expensive brands of watches show." She smiled. I felt sad thinking about their state but I needed to understand and change myself first.

I do like certain brands and wear some more than others but to me, good quality and reasonable price along with elegance and dignity is very important.

Those who can afford and consider big names and brands, I have nothing against them but just that it's not a priority for me especially when I have such tough battles to fight, when my money needs to be spent in most places early in my career.

Personal branding mattered to me

Most people want to start with and focus on materialistic branding where goods define them but I wanted to start with personal branding and then align all other areas of my life along that.

Personal branding included identifying my areas of expertise, my professional titles, the causes I worked for, the people in my tribe, who my best friend is, the people I work with, the places I would visit or be found at or met people at, the activities I did, the person I chose to marry, the kind of organization I work for, the kind of businesses that I build, the type of leaders who work in the company, , the values and principles I practice and uphold in private and public space.

Richness and Greatness

Richness of soul and sole are often closely related to greatness. In my case, I felt that a great family, great house, great car, great wedding ceremony did not mean I was great.

A lot of people feel happy, proud and great just having a connection or relation with ancestry and inheritance. I knew as a girl and due to my background and lack of certain experiences, it would be very difficult but I wanted to start and see what happens. I wanted to be known for who I am, for what I did and will do, for what I contributed and am contributing and not for my ancestors or elders greatness alone.

REFLECT:

1. What kind of richness can you most identify with, especially in your own life? Which kind of richness have you given more priority to, so far in life?

2. After reading this chapter on "Inspiration 11," what are your insights on the two kinds of richness and what will be your action plan to increase both kinds of richness?

XII
WOD & MOD

Woman of Dreams (WOD) and Man of Dreams (MOD)- this is the greatest concern for parents and family, the topic that generates a lot of excitement and interest among the youth, the area of life that society wants to have maximum dominance and control over, the topic that brings lots of pain or pleasure.

This is also an area of life that most people give a lot of thought to but that effort goes to waste, majority of the times because of lack of clarity, purpose and messed up thought and action processes involved in it, dictated by society.

Why Woman of Dreams mattered to me?

My TEDx talk speaks about my becoming the woman of my dreams. I said yes to myself, yes to my dreams, yes to becoming the woman of my dreams and no to society at 23. Why? I was fed up of that average tag that had been associated with me for a long time, everywhere and the suffering accompanied with it.

I didn't want to end up being an average woman with an average man and average marriage.

Society kept emphasizing that once you took the dive, there was no turning back, that it was important to marry and "marry well." I started becoming aware of the actual importance of marriage and "marrying well" but not society's way.

I realised that from her teens, a girl is exposed to fairy tales and books, movies and society's talks about marriage and finding love, about being perfect to attract the "right man" for marriage, to focus on being everything a potential man rather his family would want in a woman and then have a perfect "happy ever after."

I was worried that society only emphasized on the quest for love but not at all on the quest for purpose, in case of a woman, in particular.

I felt helpless, hopeless and sleepless thinking of the tragedy that had been going on for years and that would go on if I didn't take the road not taken, if I didn't show the world what was possible. I felt responsible to myself, God and humanity.

I felt it was not only my own story but the story of thousands of other girls and boys, of families and generations. There was so much suffering as a result of keeping silent on things that mattered more. I wanted to be the change not just lead the change. I had many fears.

I was concerned about the future risks, of "being miserable for not following society's path and way" or for "letting my parents and family down and seeing them suffer." I was also scared that I'd end up "not having a partner and soulmate in my youth and old age," that I'd have to "eventually settle for less."

Why Man of Dreams mattered to me?

In spite of society telling me that "perfect" isn't possible, that of one in a million get the perfect match, that if I "wait for too long" then after a certain "age" I would not get the "perfect man" and that I would feel sorry, I didn't want to listen to society. There was no way I would settle for less.

I'd rather take the risk earlier, not give in and focus on being the right woman of my dreams. I'd rather focus on being a rare breed, on striving to be a 1 in a million woman and due to persistence, good intentions, loyalty to the unseen and unknown man of my dreams, God will send the right man for me, the man of my dreams and for my dreams. He will be a rare breed of a man, also striving to be one in a million kind of a man.

I had this confidence and faith in God because I was striving hard to be the change, my vision and mission was clear and different from most people my age, younger or older. I recall how respected elders in my family, relatives or community, my teachers since school and college, men and women my age group, parents of other youth, social changemakers spoke of me.

I knew I had put in that intention, focus and grind to be who I am, to create my own identity and therefore God would definitely help especially because of my purpose and reason behind love or marriage or life's purpose.

My man of dreams couldn't just be anyone society or any "wise, caring and experienced" person chose for me "with my permission." I was serious about personal branding because I was too serious about purpose and legacy. No one could just be called "Mr. Madiha Ahmed."

I would need to be sure about the person's purpose and principles aligning or closely complementing with mine, life goals and relationship goals, health goals and family goals, personal and professional goals.

For me, marrying a man with a good list- 1,2,3,4,5 wasn't good enough, ticking off society's checklist for me. I would not allow it.

Marriage was not just a cultural, physical or societal thing for me. Marriage according to me is sacred and beautiful and great but after clarity.

It would not just affect my future but also the future of humanity.

Comparing Society's Idea of Woman of Dreams vs mine

Thinking about my life and the people I met and spoke to, I felt women were mostly of three kinds- Rebel, Robot or Reformer.

A Rebel is someone who opposes anything and everything in the name of rights or women empowerment, who will go to extremes to not think practical about circumstances, who will take negative advantage of being a woman.

A Robot is someone who does anything and everything without any objections or questions at all, consciously or unconsciously, who will go to the extremes of not thinking for herself or acting for herself, who will let others take advantage of her or they would take advantage of her.

A Reformer is someone who does what's true to herself, God and humanity irrespective of whether she wants it or society does. To her, justice and truth, being raw and real, sincerity and transparency are more important than anything. She could appear as Rebel or Robot at different times but she has it sorted internally about her "why." She strives for balance in her personality and life, thinking for herself to serve humanity, thinking for humanity and preserving herself. She is someone ready to try and learn, accept her mistakes, do better, to try and understand others and be empathetic. She is solution-oriented and action-oriented.

Society's idea of WOD is mostly a Robot that sometimes creates Rebels or a Rebel that turns into a Robot. This harms the woman herself and humanity at large. My idea of WOD is a Reformer which I'm striving to be since class 8 but with more focus and energy since 23.

Society wants a woman to follow and obey its orders, compromise everything including who she is, be inexpressive as she needed to "stay in her limits" or "know her place in the eyes of people and God." Society wants a woman to be a damsel in distress and wait for Prince Charming or a Hero to protect her from the miserable life she was/is having due to society or herself.

She is expected to control her husband or herself, always appear to be a perfect woman when nothing seems to be close to perfect even.

I believe that a woman needs to obey no one but God, not parents, not in-laws, not spouse or society. She only needs to do what God created her for and what He wants her to do.

A Reformer woman is respectful and works ethically, has productive and meaningful relationships, with higher vision and purpose in mind in all spheres of life- with her parents, her in-laws, her spouse, her children and strive for balance in personal and professional life and relationships.

I believe that she needs to be true to God and herself, to serve Him and humanity which will lead to a happy life and a life of contentment. I believe that a woman may compromise up to a certain limit and depending on situations, never compromising on values and principles because a lot of times society makes her do otherwise and she gives in often.

In relationships, there needs to be transparency so that there is no hidden "agenda," so that both parties are aware of their roles and rights while having a talk during times of conflict. At different times and situations, different people could take a lead and have a say. There could be a weekly or monthly meetup or call to invest in relationships that matter, so that the family is closely knit and misunderstandings removed.

Peaceful and United Families will lead to Peaceful and United India and World.

I believe a woman must be expressive to be able to voice her thoughts and concerns for herself, her family and humanity, not just complain or be angry and frustrated but express in a manner that gives her courage and confidence to seek the help and support she needs.

I believe that a woman first needs to be the woman of her dreams, with clarity about her life or at least started the journey to explore if not figured out yet. She needs to be solving her own problems, rescuing herself, protecting herself, taking responsibility for her own life rather than depending on a man or society.

Unless she does this for a considerable time, she will not develop the confidence, courage or clarity about life.

After she has experienced a high dose of the independence phase (even for a short duration but a high dose with a balanced and stable attitude), she can start practicing more of interdependence with other women and men.

That helps her to appreciate as well as truly understand the struggles and success of individual stories of men and women, thus helping her to identify and start figuring out the man of her dreams at some point, to be more empathetic towards people around, to serve humanity better, to do better at work and life, in business and charity.

I believe that a woman needs to only control herself and her life and no one else.

She may suggest, advice, mentor, be a friend or partner to her husband, kids or family but never dictate them as just like her, they too are created by God and to obey Him. Sometimes when kids are still young or when during her turn to support her husband, she may have to go the extra mile and be firm like her husband or kids would too if need be, some other time.

However, this needs to be done with a lot of thought, after renewing her intentions before God on why it is being done, with proper consideration and understanding of the situation and the soul, not going overboard and overwhelming them.

A Reformer Woman in case she ends up going overboard will have the courage to say sorry and reduce that behaviour or reaction the next time.

It is so sad that society only teaches and focuses on training that includes cooking, cleaning and child-rearing while leaving young women and men unequipped to face life challenges, to overcome them and be better human beings.

Society won't lead by example nor give young men and women training from good examples or striving souls. It's sad that she is not given knowledge or tools before, during or after marriage to deal with new phases.

I am already working on this to help more and more young women and men with successful and happy souls contributing to the progress of their countries and humanity.

Comparing Society's Idea of Man of Dreams vs Mine

All that I mentioned above in society's idea of WOD vs mine could be applied to that of MOD and vice-versa.

Looking back at life, I think about all the men I have seen or spoken to since childhood, I felt most were dominating towards females, disobedient in early years of their life and then becoming obedient when it required them to speak up, settling for little, being demanding of females especially.

A Rebel is someone who will have his way no matter what, without thinking of others feelings, thinking being a man makes him powerful and capable of anything in a negative sense- thinking, saying and doing what he wants, with no concern for ethics or humanity.

A Robot is someone who will do anything his "beloved" people tell him- be it parents or wife or others, not processing the information or their words or actions, believing everything they do is good and right, forgetting every soul can err. Forgetting that wrong is wrong no matter who does it.

A Reformer man knows what he wants and why. If odds are against him then he will figure out with courage and confidence due to clarity in spite of hidden fears. He knows that no soul is perfect and people may not be bad but they could be culturally driven or pressurized, therefore they make wrong decisions, losing sight of the big picture.

A Reformer man remembers his purpose and dreams, renews his intentions during turbulent times in his soul, in his family, country or world. That gives him the energy to act better and create a bigger impact, to act with empathy, truth and justice.

He reminds himself that a woman is his partner in cause, not crime, that he can cry before her and express his fears and concerns, that she could be his friend first and not just someone he looks for sex or satisfying his sexual urges through eyes or body.

He reminds himself that he is accountable to God for his thoughts, words and actions. That being a man, society might excuse him or give him privileges but before God, he is equally accountable like a woman is.

He recalls the big picture when peers or society might "allow him" to enjoy being a man or "live his life his way" or force him to "be a man" through domestic or sexual abuse or illegal sex or any other immoral actions.

A Reformer man enjoys his life "within limits" but believes in living a life of purpose, thinking anything is possible, that there are no limits, that he needs to be a man of his dreams first and then God will send him the woman of his dreams.

Love and Marriage

Society keeps emphasizing that a perfect match is impossible, that finding a man or woman of dreams is impossible or rare. They fear that if a man or a woman makes the tough choice, takes risks then he or she will "end up guilty" and no one would marry them.

It is true that most men and women are average in the world and it's a choice they've made but what if more and more of them decided to be their own MOD or WOD?

God will make the perfect match happen.

I remember telling these words to an aunt: "Majority of women are the same and typical kind which is why society wants that kind. Those women who are different, the rarer and fewer ones are thus targeted in spite of being reformers. But what if I changed my story, shared my story and inspired more women to change theirs? Would men stop marrying? Would men remain single?

No! They would have to marry the kind of women otherwise perceived as a threat to society (because they spoke up and stood up to protect society from itself.) Also, when men started changing their stories as I'm already getting that feedback through my work then men and women will find the spouse of their dreams."

I along with concerned changemakers globally are striving hard to be the change and lead the change.

Based on my story, my experiences and insights during this journey, I'm creating projects, offering services, doing research to help transform more lives, to help more men and women to say yes to their dreams and becoming their own WOD or MOD, to fulfill their life's purpose.

Marriage according to me is a way of serving God and humanity in a bigger way.

It is a way for me to increase impact for a better world for all.

Through my own, I aspire and I will strive to set new standards, be a trendsetter, share my struggles and success to help others. I am learning to equip myself to excel and do well in that phase from now since 23.

I want to help instill the faith that people have lost in marriage, when meaning and purpose of relationships and marriage itself has changed so much leading to suffering or evil.

I cannot settle for less because I am responsible and accountable to myself and God. I am not perfect but striving hard in each stage and area of life since 23 because I don't want to be average, I want to be the stereotype breaker, the trendsetter so that more people find hope and meaning in life, so that more people can live happy and content lives while being proud of their struggles and success, living with purpose and dignity, serving their families, communities, cities, countries and humanity in a bigger and better way.

Love is not just romantic moments that are portrayed by serials and dramas, books and movies.

It's impossible to spend days after days, every moment thinking of just your loved one, being with them and romancing, showing love through materialistic gifts or superficial ways or sex, showing concern through messages, calls or presence. Doing these all the time doesn't necessarily reflect love.

True love is when you give the other person the space they need while letting them know through words and actions that they can approach you and you are there.

True love is when you strive hard to be full so that your loved one can experience fullness. An example could be in the case of financial independence when a woman strives for or is financially stable and is the woman of her dreams then society will not pressurize the man or prevent him from fulfilling his dreams and from being the man of his dreams.

Society often talks of the better half but I believe both must strive for wholeness as much as possible. That both must complement each other, be a support and strength for each other through strengthening their own selves.

There are ideas in the minds of youth and even elders that opposites attract and the same kind repel. That's a fantasy according to me and lasts for some time. Marriages where couples are opposite take a lot more to be understanding and adjusting amidst life challenges- individually as well as in marriage. Even in love marriages or arranged, I've seen a lot of conflicts, people not talking or leaving homes due to frustration or a situation leading to a bad scene followed by divorce. It could lead to a lot of conflict and suffering, leaving both the husband and wife in misery, children and families suffering.

At the end, I realized, unless you are happy, you cannot make anyone else happy. So if separation and divorce brings that purpose and happiness to all concerned or to the ones that know their place or purpose in the world, in the history of humanity, in the history they can create for a better world, be it. It will bring peace in the big picture.

According to me, marriage lasts longer and is healthier when the man and the woman have things in common, the more the better as it will help them to unite and come on common terms during arguments or tough times. It will help them to enjoy and feel happy doing what they love together and not get bored or irritated often, to have more understanding of each other's lives and challenges- in personal and professional areas of life.

It is important that the man and the woman have similar principles and values in life, vision and mission, life goals and aspirations. They both must have the love for God and humanity first and then country.

They must strive hard to serve God, humanity and their country, to strive to be man or woman of their own dreams, being themselves and living a life and being the person they would want their future spouse to be.

It's unfair to live a reckless life, a purposeless life and then expect or want a spouse who is completely opposite.

I believe if you play your part well with good intentions, perseverance and faith in God then miracles will happen. You will start identifying characteristics you're looking for in a spouse in different people.

But you must not hurry or worry. Until you feel that you are ready, do not commit, do not say yes or no.

I believe it's difficult to know who your MOD or WOD is if you've not become WOD or MOD yourself or at least have made some progress to become your MOD or WOD. You'll just know and feel ready and God will give signs if you keep striving sincerely. Take advice from your parents and do things with their blessings. Discuss with them and be a great example as a son or daughter! But remember purpose over anything and anyone!

Interaction with the opposite gender

It's sad how society paints the wrong ideas and concepts on interaction with the opposite gender and forces you to stay silent rather than being honest and facing reality. That is why so many crimes happen and so much suffering occurs.

Society likes to play games, plot secret agendas, play hide and seek, speak and act with "sugar coating" and "makeup" mentality to conceal the truth. Rather than helping kids and youth to understand gender roles and interaction in a productive way, society wants to not talk about it at all, to rather have misinterpretations and misunderstandings than clarity and peace.

When a proposal doesn't work out, families stop talking like it's a huge setback or "rejection" in life, people talk bad of the same people they couldn't stop praising at some point of time. This is complete hypocrisy that bothered me.

I believe every social changemaker is part of my global tribe of changemakers and if needed you must work with them, interact and learn from them. The ultimate picture and goal is the greater good for humanity while preserving goodness in individuals and giving good a chance through combined efforts.

Men and women must work together as allies, partners, collaborators, mentors, mentees, in personal and professional space with proper knowledge of challenges that might arise and talk through them while arriving at solutions and through mutual understanding and empathy during interactions.

The world will not be a better place if only women are empowered or only men are empowered with education, counseling, a sense of purpose and economic empowerment.

Both need to work side by side so that they both develop a better understanding of the opposite gender rather than someone they only do romance with, have sex with, have sexual desires and urges for. When they study and work side by side, along with seeing good role models at home then they will learn to respect the opposite gender more and have a better understanding of their nature, thought process, work style, strengths and weaknesses thereby making better decisions for marriage and likely to have a happy one as is society's main goal and most important item on their checklist for a man or a woman.

When a proper education on gender interaction is imparted and practiced then fears of society related to it will vanish too.

I am working on this as part of my work through research followed by workshops and other initiatives.

It is important that you look at everyone as a soul first and then gender during interactions. I was made aware of this by an aunt, Gazelle Khan, who also encouraged me to not give up and work for all souls and humanity, as earlier I was working with and for women only. On following her advice, not only did I grow and benefit but so did many men and women.

Many a time, I've received comments and messages from men asking for help and the problems or concerns are what I knew existed but were not spoken about. I rarely responded when at 23 as I am still researching. When I posted my article on "Human Spices," a boy commented that if I as a girl could change my story, so could he. He asked me what he should do and I told him to wait for this book!

I have had and presently have some very productive and meaningful relationships with men over the last years since 23 and that too globally, virtual and in-person, all of which have been a win-win situation and great learning experiences. I realized that it is up to us women to set the standards and choose how you want to be treated. So many times they would not call me by name due to respect. Some would call me Didi meaning elder sister or ma'am, Ms. Madiha or even Madiha (as "aap" for you).

Those who called me Madiha without the respectful "aap," I gave a clear indication I didn't like jokes nor understood them. Those who tried to be friendly with decent manners but calling me like they would do to other friends or how cool people talk whether male or female, I would object and they would say sorry.

One thing I realized on many occasions was that the way I dressed gave me this kind of respect from men and women, young and old, educated and uneducated, modern and traditional, along with my striving for what I believed in and to not be average, to be focused and sincere.

I knew in every place, God wanted me to lead and be an example and I did do my best. That helped me understand that it was possible to stand out in any place in spite of the "not so cool or modern clothes, without makeup and fake accent."

There were 2-3 occasions when during weddings young men either came up to me or my family members introducing themselves as my friend or telling me where they met me. I felt like they felt the pride to have seen, met or heard me. I added my father and family on Facebook, posted pictures and videos of me, interacted with and tagged men. I knew my parents and family and even relatives were observing. That way they knew where I was going, who I was meeting, what my activities were and how I interacted with them.

When a boy comments a simple thing like nice or on my pictures, I delete their comments or question them why they had to comment unnecessarily. I don't check or respond to my inbox messages until I feel right or get a positive vibe. It is important to set the tone, the rules and clarify when the need arises so that the conversation stays productive and meaningful.

This doesn't mean that conversations were always very crisp or rude. Many a time they were personal and very dignified, productive and impactful. This according to society isn't possible but I knew it was.

It felt great to see how young male and female change-makers were breaking stereotypes and proving they were more ethical than the society they grew up in. I truly feel blessed and honoured to know, learn and work with such great souls with such focus.

REFLECT:

1. Are you a Rebel, Robot or Reformer? Why do you categorize yourself as such?

2. What action will you take after reading this chapter on "Inspiration 12" to go to the next level and improve yourself?

XIII

What Awakens you?

When I shared a Google form on Facebook for people to ask me questions on dreams or my life while being anonymous, many people had questions like what was my dream that led to such transformation in my life or brought such success, how can a person know about their life purpose, how to start the journey towards saying yes to dreams or becoming man or woman of your own dreams and many other questions.

Through this book, I have covered almost all the questions and shared my journey with the world. There was a time when I thought I knew what my dream was. I heard people talking of chasing their dreams.

I realized that most people think they know their dreams but the truth is that most do not.

Most people either allow others to tell them what to do and how to do or they prefer to go with the flow or they think dreams don't come true so why think about them.

Some are afraid of the big changes and coming out of their comfort zone. Some feel lazy thinking of all the hard work involved. Some think they will think about it when they have time and freedom from a 9 to 5 job.

I have seen a trend in the older generation, my parents generation and generations before that where they had a dream to "see their parents or elders happy" by obeying them in everything- in the choices of study, work, marriage, lifestyle, car and food. Almost everything.

It didn't matter what they wanted, what made them happy, what would make the world a better place. Those generations when they see my generation and the ones after that then they say: "These "kids" don't understand. The world has turned so bad. In our time we did what our parents told us. We never had the concept of choice."

To me, these words feel like they are trying to appear happy by that choice they allowed to be made on their behalf, it seemed like they were trying to show it to be a good thing but there is always this slight give away by almost all of them that I have picked up. They also feel unhappy and guilty thinking about it later on in life. Maybe they were wishing they had the courage to do it.

Sometimes I have also seen the vicious cycle being repeated of "I was not allowed to do it" or "I did it this way" or "This is how it was done." But I'm glad to see cases where parents have supported their children and supported their dreams right from the start or sometimes eventually supporting it even if they did not have the choice to do or were "not allowed in their time."

The majority have no clarity of dreams and purpose due to various reasons. The problem with most people is that they set small average goals, sometimes the goals are so low and simple and easy that they reach it easily.

Many a times you may reach your goal and be so happy, excited and satisfied that you want to be celebrating that state and stage for a long time. You stop challenging yourself to dream big and to take your life to the next level, to realize your soul's, your life's true potential.

I had told myself this: "Madiha, you have within you great, unrealized, unutilized treasures waiting to be discovered, developed, demonstrated to make your life and the world better. How can you settle for little, for mediocrity, to be the average student in this test of life? Are you not fed up being average all your life? Have you not been an all-rounder at school? Why not in life?"

When I heard too many things about me, I would tell myself: "Madiha, you are not the observations people have made of you. You are not the character others have painted of you. You are the character you choose to be. You won't let society dictate and let your life be governed, dominated and destroyed by their checklist (a general common, poor, "standard" checklist they have for every person.) You have to traverse the road not taken. Start, take the risk. See what happens. Maybe you will fail big time. Or maybe make it bigger than you or anyone ever imagined. Give it a shot."

What are Dreams?

I think dreams are the goals and plans I write down in my diary about what I want to do with my life, updating them as I grow each day in knowledge and experiences about myself, others and the world around me.

Dreams are the visions and scenes I see myself in, see myself in action- doing them a few minutes, hours, days, weeks, months or years from now.

Dreams are plans I want to accomplish no matter how hard and hopeless or high and hopeful life gets. Dreams make me sleep peacefully and sleep enough so that I stay fresh, that I'm awake to live the life I deserve.

Dreams awaken me to who I am, they awaken me to the people and the world around me.

Dreams for me are actions that will make me and the around me better, that will reduce suffering and evil in the world, that will bring unity, justice, peace and progress for all.

Here are a few things associated with dreams:

1. Fright

Dreams can scare you.

The possibility of your dreams coming true or not coming true can frighten you. This fear could be due to your loved ones, family, relatives or society trying to talk you out of it. It could also be due to the risks involved or uncertainty like: "What if I failed after putting a lot of efforts?" or "What if I lost everything including what I have?" or "What if people mock me and criticise me when I fail?" Even today I have these kinds of thoughts but the frequency has decreased a lot.

The way I deal with it today is by telling myself: "What if I make it and accomplish? I will have everything I wanted and what I deserve!" or "What if I get everything I ever dreamt of and beyond my expectations if I don't give up?" or "What if my success changes the attitude and who knows the hearts of people?"

Working at Lifebushido, it had become my daily habit to feel "Anything is Possible!" I listen to motivational talks on YouTube, read articles or talk to inspiring people when I feel scared, when I feel fear gripping me. I find some songs by Britt Nicole, Toby Mac, Jason Gray, Casting Crowns, Owl City, Francesca Battistelli, Natalie Grant, Mandisa, Jasmine Murray very inspiring, when scared or worried about life or future.

I listened to motivational talks on legacy, never giving up, miracles, success, vision, hard work, problems, easy, strong, gift, life, responsibility, decision and so on. I used to pray to God often looking at the sky and telling Him my fears, requesting for strength and help while striving hard personally and publicly in all areas of life.

One of the ways I found to overcome fears is to do something that makes you feel accomplished. I would take out my diary and get done whatever

I could or try and help someone that would lead to appreciation. Both of these would make me hopeful and energized, to stop thinking about impossibilities and focus on possibilities.

Let your faith be bigger and scare your fears!

2. Height

Living your dreams and fulfilling them will take your life to the next level of physical, mental, emotional, social, economic and spiritual well-being.

It will enhance the quality and quantity of life, your way of living, of existing. It will make you thrive, not just survive.

The journey you go through will refine your soul to make it shine brighter and the struggles will purify your soul if you choose and allow that to happen.

When you decide to say yes to dreams that will be the first step towards starting your climb and ascending the mountain to reach the top and conquer it.

You are not going to make it big immediately but eventually.

I made a lot of small goals that resulted in long daily or weekly to-do lists, some of which I completed and some carried onto the next day or week but as I did or did not do, I got more clarity on how to make things simpler, crisper and organized, on having more focus to get work accomplished, to find and explore resources, to make my own notes, develop my own insights, to seek help wherever needed.

On one hand, there were small goals and on the other there were very big goals that seemed impossible but on closing eyes and visualizing them, to see myself in action, I was spurred to act on the list of small goals.

Dreaming big is not enough, you must plan and do big with powerful intentions for big impact.

3. Light

Dreams help me to shed light on the purpose of my life.

Dreams are a source of direction in life- to take you to all the places you have never been to, to feel the emotions and the experiences you have never felt, to meet the people you have never met, to witness and see the miracles you have never seen or witnessed or imagined or expected.

Imagine not living a life of your dreams could deprive you of so many great things. I don't think there was any one moment that helped me to figure out my life's purpose. There were many moments and I am sure there will be many more to help me get more clarity over the years.

I would ask myself questions like:

What is it that I love doing so much that I can do it if someone asked me to do it, waking me up from sleep?

When 1 die, what do I want to be remembered for? How will people remember me and for what?

What problems do I want to solve in the world? What are those problems that I see and tell myself: "I wish I could do something to solve it?"

What if there were no limitations or challenges in life like family or society objecting, fear of failure and I had all the resources I needed, what would I do? What would I think and plan?

Describe yourself in 3-5 words. Doing this exercise I realized who I was, what I wanted to be known for.

There may be a lot of exercises and questions to help you start figuring out your life's purpose. You can try and see which works best for you and helps you get clarity.

4. Might

Dreams will give you might, strength to fight the battles that need to be fought and that matter more rather than fighting each and every battle in life, thereby wasting your precious thought, time and effort.

They will give you strength to live, live for something larger than yourself and your life, so that you don't waste your precious life, talents and resources, leading to unproductivity and unhappiness.

Courage is not easy at all when your purpose brings clarity, when that affects your behaviour and actions, that troubles and bothers people around you, that makes them very concerned about your well-being or due to society's reaction to you.

The challenges you face on the way to achieving your dreams will strengthen your soul.

When I wanted courage, I would indulge in positive self-talk, reminding myself of the past where I overcame struggles, that bothered me earlier were insignificant today, that bad times pass quickly too.

I would renew my intentions, forcing me to think about my "why" when needing courage, talking to God about how my "why" was more powerful than the side that was trying to dominate me.

I would tell God that I was striving to be different from the society from those who were trying to talk me out of my dreams. I would tell God that I will make different choices and that I have been making them with His help.

I told God: "I am choosing mastery over misery. I am choosing purpose and passion over pain. I am choosing diligence over the dilemma. I am choosing resilience over regret. I am choosing legendary over laziness. I am choosing hard work over helplessness and hopelessness. I am choosing amazing over average."

My soul was fed up with average. I could hear it say: "Madiha, enough of average. You don't deserve it. You will not settle for it. You deserve more. You will win. Go for your dreams and reach for the mountains and stars. You need to go to the mountains to get the top view, the real and the big picture of the world you want to serve. You need to climb and conquer the mountains as they are assigned by God to you. He knew that you will conquer them and help others climb and conquer their own dreams. Madiha, you need to reach the stars, explore the big and beautiful world for the benefit of mankind and its progress."

5. Sight

Dreams will give you the vision to see things, plan things and do things ahead of your time. A friend of mine, Tapan Aslot from Bangalore who is a filmmaker shared something on problems in life during our conversation: "Close up is when you are too close to the subject. You can't see a lot of things but just the subject. If you pull your camera a little back, it's mid-close-up. You'll start seeing other supporting elements as well. Pull back more. It's a long shot. You'll see a much clearer picture and lots of other elements to consider. Extreme long shot is the wider-most perspective, where you see past-present-future. At this point, you have the full view of all the stuff you are dealing with. You have the library to keep and remove as you please. It's your film. Decide what to keep and what to remove. Then decide how much close you want to get full close up, mid-close-up, long or extreme long."

With big dreams, struggles will also be big, challenges will be big, the barriers will be big. To deal with them, I felt I needed to have a clear vision and mission in life. I needed a way to deal with challenges, internal and external.

My soul tribe, my mentors and friends, the courses helped me get clarity, improve my vision so that my dreams are at the forefront of my thoughts, words and actions, so that I see the world through the sight of my dreams.

I didn't want to feel hopeless but keep striving, so that I see my dreams through the sight of the world and its needs to make it better and to serve humanity and God better using my talents and gifts.

6. Right

Dreams will lead to God helping you to make everything right for you and others eventually.

Dreams will help you realize your true potential, to help you do what's best for you and others, to have the life you want and that you know you deserve.

You will not feel like doing something sometime, which is perfectly human. You must do something every day and if one task is difficult due to struggles or mood or health issues, do what is possible, make some progress each day.

I have discovered, learned and developed some insights on dreams over the last few years:

Dream about your days, not daydream!

Dreaming about success in business, love, relationships, education is not wrong. However, if it becomes a habit, no actions but an obsession or addiction then beware. It will take you far away from reality and create chaos in your present world, eliminating your chances of "happily ever after!"

Dreaming during the day won't help you. Dreaming and Doing about your days to come will help you.

Dream about the days to come. Imagine the life you have always wanted to live, things you always wanted to do and let that motivate you, to drive you to actions that will reflect your focus and determined attitude.

Have a focused mind that can ward off distractions and filter them.

Dreams must drive you. Imagine a driver who is not focused. He can cause accidents and be a danger to himself and others.

Dreams can drive you to be adventurous, not reckless, to enjoy and live the moments, to yearn for even better moments. They must not distract you to worrying or unhealthy thoughts and ideas and drift away from the reality or the present.

So dream on dreamer but watch out the time, place, occasion and environment!

Dreams awaken us, not make us sleep

Dreams that make you run away from the real world, leading to sleep, shutting off the senses and of the soul's function may not be dreams at all. They will take away your precious energy, brain space, resources that could be used to invest, create, build, establish meaning in life.

Dreams must awaken us from hibernation, the comfort zones and to our own treasures. Shake off that drowsiness, laziness and get to the real action.

Strive to look inside, at your own "status quo" and at your own SWOT so that you can turn the weaknesses into strengths and threats into opportunities.

You have great undiscovered treasures, unutilized energy, talent, resources and ideas that can change your world and our world.

You are not aware and are not using it.

Imagine all the possibilities if you gather the courage to use them. Are you going to waste all the precious treasure?

The choice is yours! Do not complain later that you don't have what it takes to dream and do big.

You didn't say yes to your dreams because you thought you couldn't, you weren't capable, what will people say?

Remember your saying yes to your dreams by your beliefs and actions is more powerful than their saying no.

So, dream it, do it. Dare to dream and do.

Dreams don't work unless you do

Worrying, weeping, wandering, wishing, waiting simply, whining will not make your dreams come true.

Working, withstanding and worshiping will make your dreams come true. At times, you might have to dream big and act small.

Daily, disciplined, determined, doings lead to great results.

My Dream

So, what is my dream rather what are my dreams that got me started, that made me say yes? That still gives me the courage to keep striving, to never give up and to stay focused?

My Vision: To Think and Act Local, National and Global, working with the support of like-minded people and organizations who believe in connecting ideas and people for a Peaceful World.

My Mission: To transform lives through skill based education and economic empowerment, to increase impact and create a ripple effect.

My Why?

So what is it that drives me to say what I say, to do what I do, to be who I am every single day?

1) Continuing the legacy of my fore-"fathers"

My great-grandfathers and grandfathers from the paternal and the maternal side were actively involved in social work.

My paternal great-grandfather, Mohammed Suleiman Vawda, who adopted my grandfather, was an author of several books to clarify the common misunderstandings about my faith. He was involved in the Indian freedom movement and associated with several renowned social organizations in Kolkata that served the society.

My paternal grandfather, Late Abdul Haque Ahmed, was associated with several organizations like Calcutta Muslim Orphanage, Anjuman Khadimul Hujjaj and some others in the past.

My maternal great-grandfather, Late Noor Md Dinath, built a hospital that offered free maternal and child care in Surat, built a home in the suburbs during my great-grandmother's illness for her treatment and then opened the space for others going through the same.

My maternal grandfather, Late Yusuf Dinath, when he passed away in October 2017 and his body was being taken to the grave, the people on the road shut down the lights and stood up in respect. His funeral was attended by hundreds of people and a big number turned up to tell my grandmother how generous he was. We did not know that he had touched so many lives in a big way.

One day, during my visit in early 2017, when my nana (maternal grandfather) was undergoing oral cancer treatment, I was seeking his advice and then I told him that to me legacy was not about carrying on the name of the family or owning the property and materialistic richness.

I believed that legacy was about holding on, passing on the values and principles that were beneficial for humanity, from one generation to the next. It was not a "male thing." I take legacy seriously as I have to level up the game of my family and create bigger and deeper impact so that I can be a means of on-going charity for my fore-"fathers" and fore-"mothers" and for my parents.

2) Social Work and Business

In the last 6-8 years, I have seen a lot of people around me either doing business well or charity well. Rarely, have I seen people around me doing "ethical charity" and "ethical business"- both well.

When I came across, Social Entrepreneurship 101 course from +Acumen, I realized I wanted to use my heart and brain – both to the fullest and effectively to leave a legacy, create impact and grow and evolve along with the world. I will continue to strive to be an example. I will strive to stay authentic and true to God and myself. I am building businesses in diverse domains with social impact at its core and non-profits that can sustain themselves and the people leading them.

3) Giving the world a glimpse into the mind of an empowered woman and telling her side of the story.

While exploring potential spouse for marriage and what other girls have shared of their story over the last few years, I identified concerns that the boy's side has regarding an empowered woman.

I realized that the world has hardly heard her and known a truly empowered woman who is not a curse, a family-breaker, who pursues unnecessary "hobbies and interests" when her father and husband can easily provide for her!

I want to give the world a glimpse into the mind of such a woman through my TEDx Talk and through my book, through my work and the life I am striving for.

I want to be remembered as a soul that gave good a chance. I want to be remembered as a soul that got fed up of being average, who made a choice to make herself better to make the world better.

4) Better Me, Better India, Better World

I realized India was average because I was average for so long. I wanted to shine so that India could shine. I will continue to strive to shine so that India shines!

I realized that there was lack of peace and unity in the world and in my country, India because it was lacking in families. I started working effectively as a Parent and Youth Mentor and Teacher Trainer and my vision aligned with Dr.A.P.J Abdul Kalam. I believed working with these three powerful forces would lead to a Better India.

In addition to that I will continue to strive to improve myself so that a Better Me will lead to a Better India and a Better World.

5) The Edu Doctor

During the Edu Cafe 2022 in Dubai, it felt great to be called on stage as a speaker as The Edu Doctor from India.

I started off with education as part of my purpose and calling, I wanted to be a neurosurgeon, God had better plans. After spending 10+ years in education, while I was striving to be the woman of my dreams and serving my family, my country and humanity to the best of my ability, I ended up decoding the doctor part of The Edu Doctor.

It is in July, 2022, when I am editing my book to finally publish it, I am grateful to God and glad to share that while God gave me the opportunity to serve my Late grandfather, my dada, Abdul Haque in his last days on earth, when I worked from the hospital on all my dreams and responsibilities, being beside him all day, talking to doctors and health experts at GD Hospital, Kolkata that I found the missing piece because I chose purpose.

A lot of people would be curious at work or my team or clients, relatives and strangers- why would a professionally successful woman do this? You see it was the society's checklist that had the problem, not mine. I knew my purpose as a strong, independent and successful woman, as people like to call it.

I wanted my grandfather to have that one female in his life, in his last part of life who did not leave him, who loved him, who gave consistent care because men deserve love, men deserve care and appreciation, men matter. Together, healed men and healed women can heal humanity. Together, my papa and I, we broke the stereotypes related to gender and intergenerational challenges. We healed humanity through our example.

He would talk less as he had difficulty talking or breathing but through holding my hands, his eyes movement, his facial movements, he conveyed a lot. I feel honoured and privileged to have spent so much time, so closely with him, understanding how to take his legacy forward. It grieves me to think he is no more to love me and pray for me, to guide me and to say he is proud of me as he would often say. But in those last few days of his life, I realized he trained me and guided me in the way forward in all areas of my life. I realized what a legend he is, he led fearlessly by example, in his youth years raising his voice and in his old age through his deep and wise silence that I got inspiration from.

It helped to take care of him at the hospital as I came from a biology background and talking to doctors and experts helped to understand how to care for my grandpa the best way possible. Some would ask if I came from a medical background and I would say: I could not fulfill the dream as I had planned but it turned out better. There were occasions when he would not cooperate with doctors but let me do it easily.

I learnt through the help and guidance of a mentor, Mr. Arif Hossain, my papa's cardio-respiratory physiotherapist at GD Hospital, about geriatrics and was inspired to start the foundations of AH Elderly care when we discussed papa's condition in detail.

And this is how my life story in this book ends. The "perfect" ending, with the blessings of my papa of me finding purpose and figuring out the edu and doctor part of THE EDU DOCTOR.

REFLECT:

1. How would you define dreams? What is your dream?

2. What action will you take after reading this chapter on "Inspiration 13" to live a life that you are proud of and that you can proudly say: "I said yes to my dreams. I said yes to becoming the man or woman of my dreams?"

CONCLUSION

In my life, I've come across two kinds of people that made me reflect and inspired me to think and plan my life in a balanced way.

The "imperfect type" thought: "I am going to Hell anyway. I am proud to be bad! Who cares. I will do what I like."

The "perfect type" thought: "I am perfect. I can make no mistakes. Nothing is wrong with me."

No one is perfect.

As a human being, just like you do good, there will be times when you will do bad things too. You will make mistakes and mess up things.

What separates great from the average is how you deal with that mistake, how you choose to respond.

Inspiration is everywhere.

Be open to receiving it with an open mind and open heart by being present, by being mindful and conscious.

Reflect on what you see or listen.

Ask yourself: "Can something better be done than the status quo?"

Ask yourself: "How can I be better than I am?"

Ask yourself: "How can I do better than I am doing?"

Strive while keeping in mind the greater good for yourself and humanity. When you do that, you will be successful in fulfilling your dreams and even transcending them through effort, powerful intentions, faith and miracles. When you feel stuck or overwhelmed then go back to being open to receive inspiration.

Inspiration is everywhere.

Instead of looking for an inspiring person, look for inspiration in every person.

Looking for a complete and perfect inspiration will be very difficult as you as a human don't know the difference between the intentions, actions, sincerity. Only God knows that!

Also, no one is perfect and flawless. To judge a person as bad because of certain mistakes which he or she has overcome or repented for is unfair, overlooking all the good or positive they may have done. We can't do that judgment. Only God can!

You need a mind-shift.

You need to learn to look at things and think about them differently.

It's time you stop thinking about yourself: "Why I Can't?" and start thinking "Why Can't I?"

An activity that really helped me in life which I included in one of my workshops was:

I learned.

I am learning.

I will learn.

I planned.

I am planning.

I will plan.

I performed.

I am performing.

I will perform.

I prayed.

I am praying.

I will pray.

I succeeded.

I am succeeding.

I will succeed.

I won.

I am winning.

I will win.

You are a human being.

God made you.

God gave you choices.

You choose if you want to feel happy or sad.

You choose if you want to spend your life feeling sorry or feeling proud.

You choose if you want to live a life of purpose or a purposeless life.

You choose whether you will allow the good and the bad in your life to spur you to act positively or negatively.

The choice is yours.

Inspiration is all around.

It's your choice to seek it.

You must have and you do have dreams and purpose in life.

It's your choice to fulfill it.

Start that quest if you have not begun yet.

It's not too late.

If you have already started then get more focused and organized as reminders and reading always helps.

If there is no clarity yet about your dreams and purpose then no problem!

Start.

Let the journey teach you while you learn from other sources too. Be open to inspiration and learning.

When the voices around you say "No" to things that matter, listen to your heart.

Tell them "No. I can't listen to you because it is not good for this heart and humanity."

God taught me through this life so far from my observations and experiences which inspires me always: "Madiha, Great people inspire others. Legends inspire themselves."

I will be that legend. I started the journey by saying yes at 23.

Epilogue

Dear readers,

You must be wondering what is next after I said no to being average, after I said yes to me, yes to becoming the woman of my dreams and saying yes to my dreams.

I realized that Peacemakers are Programmers, and that is me.

I realized that I was on a Quest: purpose, love and peace.

And that, dear readers, is what my next book is all about!

Excited for the second book, curious about what happens next?

Stay tuned!